The Modern Piano

The
Modern Piano

By

Lawrence M. Nalder

UNWIN BROTHERS LIMITED

The Gresham Press

OLD WOKING, SURREY, ENGLAND

THE MODERN PIANO by Lawrence M. Nalder
with 116 figures and diagrams

ISBN 0–905418–10–7, hardback edition
ISBN 0–905418–11–5, paperback edition

Reprinted by photolitho from the original edition of
1927

Published and printed by
UNWIN BROTHERS LIMITED
The Gresham Press, Old Woking, Surrey, GU22 9LH,
England

© UNWIN BROTHERS LIMITED 1977

PREFACE TO THIS EDITION

This is one of my favourite books, the original edition being 5 by 7½ inches (123 × 186 mm)—convenient for the pocket. Modern production methods demand this new size in order to conform with the style of a new series on instrument construction.

Rumour hath it that Lawrence Nalder diligently made copious notes at the Sydney Hurren lectures he attended with the intention of writing in the twenties a book such as this on the methods, processes and tables used in the construction of pianos to complement and to codify the knowledge hitherto passed down from father to son or apprentice.

Robert Nalder, nephew of Lawrence, has kindly given permission for the book to be re-printed, and I am indebted to him for his help in this matter and to Unwin Brothers Limited for undertaking the re-printing.

Frank W. Holland, FIMIT,
Founder & Director, the British Piano Museum Charitable
    Trust No. L.242341
Brentford, Middlesex.

INTRODUCTION TO THIS EDITION

It is common knowledge that many extraordinarily talented people have devoted their lives to the composition and performance of music intended for the piano. What is not so well known, however, is the fact that a small, but no less gifted group of people have devoted *their* lives to the design and making of the piano itself, as a physical entity. In pursuit of their vocation, such persons invariably acquire a vast store of knowledge, and some reach the point where they feel impelled to share this information with others, by writing a book.

With the exception of a few highly technical books intended for persons engaged in the trade, the majority of books on the piano attempt to cover *all* aspects, including those of which the author's knowledge may be superficial, or at best secondhand. Such a criticism could hardly be levelled at Lawrence Nalder, whose book "The Modern Piano" was first published half a century ago. Of one of Nalder's earlier books, a contemporary writer observed, "It bears the stamp of genuine knowledge and experience throughout", and this phrase might well be applied to the work presently under discussion. In spite of the rather technical nature of parts of the book, it is very readable and provides the general reader with a fascinating insight into many of the things which go into the design and making of a piano. At the same time, it contains a great deal of technical information of value to the more serious student.

Occasionally one comes across references which date the book somewhat, or statements which are at variance with present day knowledge, but the latter are commendably few. This surely says a great deal for the vision as well as the sound basic knowledge of the author, and there must be few books on the subject which contain such a wealth of information in so compact a form.

Robert Morgan, MIMIT

THE

MODERN PIANO

BY

LAWRENCE M. NALDER

Author of "Essays in Pianoforte Technology"

116 FIGURES AND DIAGRAMS

Published at the Offices of "Musical Opinion,"
13, Chichester Rents, Chancery Lane, London, W.C.

Price: Four Shillings

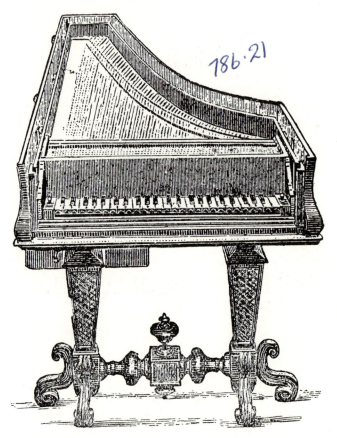

786.21

CRISTOFORI PIANO-E-FORTE: 1726
(See page 148)

*[The Cristofori action is shown
in detail on page 129, Fig. 75]*

CONTENTS

FRONTISPIECE Cristofori Piano-e-forte.

FOREWORD

CHAPTER I. Tone and Touch.

II. Quality of Tone.

III. Piano Tone compared with the Voice and Other Instruments.

Chart showing a comparison of piano compass with other instruments — essential features of all musical instruments — a detailed consideration of them in the violin, the voice, the piano.

IV. The Forms of the Piano.

The horizontal—the upright—the art piano—varied types of manufacture.

V. The Pedals.

The pedals of the grand—the pedals of the upright—the middle or tone-sustaining pedal.

VI. The Construction of the Modern Piano.

Formulæ governing string vibrations — the "scale" — the wires—scale design—a detailed scale for a grand of 172 cm. (5ft. 8in.) in length—the preparation of scale rod —the preparation of scale drawing—a scale drawing for a grand piano.

VII. The Iron Frame.

Interesting historical details — the modern frame — its appurtenances—types of frames.

VIII. The Action.

Introduction—nomenclature—essentials of action manufacture—the grand action—the upright action—compound escapement upright actions — lost motion attachments— the sostenuto attachment—setting up the action in the piano—some American actions—words and phrases used by action finishers—the history of the action—the Cristofori and other early grand and upright actions — the Erard actions—the first upright piano—the sticker action —the Wornum actions—modern actions of Brooks, Higel, &c.

CONTENTS—*Continued*

IX. The Hammer.

Cristofori's hammer — early hammers — the single and double-coated felt hammer—hammer making—the toning of hammers (practical hints).

X. The Keyboard.

Historical — early organ keyboards — the diatonic keyboard — the Halberstadt keyboards — the problems of intonation—the modern keyboard—touch—key-covering material.

XI. The Soundboard.

Sound — material for soundboards — the American "upright grand" back — recent French patents — down bearing—varnish.

XII. The Piano of the Future.

Defects of the modern piano—the Janko keyboard—the Emanuel Moor duplex-coupler piano — the quarter-tone pianos—a new German quarter-tone keyboard.

XIII. Notes on Historical and Modern Pitch Standards. The Tuning Fork.

FOREWORD

THOUGH no writer of serious intent would wish to speak lightly of any work on the piano previously published, for most of them have been our "guide, philosopher and friend" during musical adolescence, the conclusion comes at length that no one among them quite fulfils the needs of students of the modern piano as an acoustic entity. Still less does any book purporting to describe the instrument disclose much of value to men of to-day whose avocations are with pianos, be they teacher or tuner, student or seller. The principles of construction and operation of the piano are known but dimly to the public, and even many artist-performers would have a hard task to explain adequately the essential working parts of their medium.

Excluding one comprehensive book on the piano,[1] whose purpose is mainly that of construction, most of the others are overladen with matter of historical interest. The period which saw the publication of the works of Rimbault and Hipkins was a time of transition, and hence much of their contents is now archaic. Nothing on similar lines has since appeared.

It is, consequently, much to be hoped that a book which aims at an explanation of the piano as we know it to-day may be written and found worthy of reading, and perhaps of study, by those who find pianos in their path and who are ever anxious to speak within their knowledge.

London, May, 1927.

---

[1] Wolfenden's "Art of Pianoforte Construction" (1916).

1

" Music, which gentler on the spirit lies
Than tired eyelids upon tired eyes."

"The piano: what is it? It is a musical instrument of the percussion class.... A sudden impulse is given to the vibrating system, *which is then left to itself*."

Dictionary of Applied Physics.

CHAPTER I

Tone and Touch

THE piano of to-day must be regarded as the extreme development of a stringed musical instrument operated by keys. To say that the piano is a development of the harp of remote antiquity, in which the strings were plucked by the fingers, or later, of the dulcimer or spinet, are classifications far too loose.

The function of many early instruments was to assist the human voice: to provide an elemental system of accompaniment. Such accompaniments might be pitched a fourth or an octave below the voice, and moved with the melody. The organ was, about the tenth century, used as an embodiment of this idea. There exist, however, authentic records of the organ so far back as the second century B.C. The keys of the early organ had little resemblance to the clavier of our own times. It was during the fifteenth century that the size and shape of the keys took an approximately standard form. The keys of the early instruments required great power to overcome their resistance. Thus keys had to be made wide enough to be struck by the clenched fist or depressed by the whole weight of the palm of the hand. An early organ at Halberstadt Cathedral was "played by a crude and clumsy collection of chains, wires and cranks." [2]

The keyboard suffered many vicissitudes: but the discerning mind immediately appreciates the fact that the keyboard of to-

[2] " Keys and Stops," by Andrew Freeman. (Contained in No. 2 of *The Organ.*)

3

day existed and had influenced musical thought for possibly two or three centuries before the piano was born.   Bartolommeo Cristofori of Padua, about the time George I. came to the English throne (1714), was working upon his first hammer-action instrument, which came to be known as *piano-e-forte*,—that is, soft and loud.

Against a development of two thousand years, which is that of the organ, the piano has had two hundred years only in which to grow.   This comparison is instructive.   True, the piano was a natural evolution from the harpsichord, which in turn grew from the spinets and virginals of the Elizabethan era.   The clavichord developed during the fifteenth, sixteenth, seventeenth and even up to the eighteenth century.   In its ultimate state it became a musical instrument of the highest order, possessing a *Klangfarbe* that was sympathetic, even spiritual.   Bach himself, it is said, could produce exquisitely beautiful effects on a clavichord: it was a keyed instrument of sweet and limpid tone, it could express individuality, it was possessed of a soul!   Beethoven, it is recorded, preferred the delicacy of the clavichord to the heavy and harsh tones of the harpsichord and the early piano.

In the more important features of construction, the clavichord and the piano have a singular degree of resemblance. Both have metal strings, agitated by blows, both utilise a sound-board to amplify the tone.   (Pitch as well as tone were governed by the blow in the clavichord.)   The keyboards are identical, except, of course, in compass.

At this point, it will be well to attempt a definition of the piano.   Essentially it is a musical instrument of the percussion type operated by digital levers.   The source of energy is lengths of finely drawn steel wire: these are stretched at a high tension over and in contact with a "sound expander," named the sound-board, and are excited by felt-faced hammers.

With this definition before us, it is possible to examine the possibilities and the limitations of the instrument.   The maker of the piano has fixed its tone-quality almost as surely as he has fixed the pitch of each note.   Being of fixed pitch, it suffers the limitations of the "temperament" to which it is tuned.   Chief among its limiting factors, however, is the inability of the performer to vary the quality of the sound once it is produced (excluding the use of the pedals), and also the fact that the sound cannot be sustained.

The production of sound—of tone—is dependent upon such

a marvellous and harmonious working of detail, that every sound possesses an individuality. No two sisters have the same voice: no two dogs bark alike: and no two pianos have exactly identical tones. Yet the tone-quality yielded from an individual instrument is always the same. This statement may startle those who fondly imagine that tone is a matter of touch. The school of piano thumpers is almost extinct: in its place, however, we have modern exponents of touch systems of piano technique. These people claim that an entirely different type of touch produces an entirely different type of tone. They are probably quite unaware that an immense variety in quality is made possible by combinations of notes struck at intervals of a few *hundredths of a second*. The quality of tone obtained from a piano when a melody note is struck is dependent upon the body of other tones then existing from other keys previously struck *and sustained*. The quality also depends upon the length of time each of these tones has been sounding.

Physicists who have studied the subject venture the opinion that the touch of a master-artist such as Paderewski consists in very slight variations in the time of striking the different keys, as well as in the varying strength of the blow.

In point of fact—apart, of course, from pedalling—a pianist has only two variable factors at his disposal: one is the *speed of the blow*, and the second is the minute variations in the moment of attack between different notes. Speed of blow is regulated by the power expended to depress the key and drive forward the hammer to the string. Translated into piano technique: it is known as *touch*. Variations in touch-power enable a melody to be distinguished from an accompaniment. The best example of this is the accented roll for the player piano. The variation of the perforations in the music-roll controls the striking power of a pneumatic finger. One note is louder than another. There is hardly any difference in *tone colour* between a loud and a soft note. It is a matter of quantity, of volume (and so duration) rather than quality. This power of variation of loudness is ever at the disposal of the pianist: it provides the light and shade indispensable to artistic and individual interpretation of music.

The question which now arises is: How far can touch of itself affect tone quality? The writer makes bold to answer that the effect of touch on the tonal composition of a note is almost non-existent. There may be clamorous disagreement with this statement; but let the facts be considered frankly.

The clavichord note could be altered in pitch by the touch of the performer, and so also could the tone. In the modern piano, however, the length, the thickness, and the tension of the string are fixed. So also is the point of impact of the hammer, and the hardness of the hammer. The maker has decided the relative position of the bridges and the soundboard. Tone is essentially dependent on the factors enumerated. Touch gives a little or much of one tone.

If a piano is old and the hammer-felt hard, no doubt the bass (i.e., the strings with copper coverings) can be made to yield a mass of discordant overtones under heavy-handed exponents of the keyboard. But all this is beside the issue, as also is the continued use of pedals to obtain effects from resonance and repetitions of rapid dampings of the strings.

If the small variations in the time of striking a combination of notes can be categorised as touch, then it can be laid down that "touch" can vary the ultimate tonal effect of any pianoforte. But is this variation a question of touch? It must be noted that the changed and ever changing effects obtained by a great artist are due to resonance: to sympathetic vibrations from other keys which are sustained by those keys not being released; or by the use of the sustaining pedal. It is helpful to remember that when any note on the piano is struck, *every* string on the instrument is endeavouring to vibrate in sympathy, whether the dampers are pressing on the strings or whether they are quite free from them. Sympathetic vibration results in a re-arrangement of the tonal structure of one or of a combination of notes.

Moreover, tempo, rhythm, and the temperament of the performer colour the ultimate effect as well as the tone of the instrument. Even if it could be proved that the speed with which the hammer moves towards the strings *does* vary the tone, this variation can be only within a very narrow range.

The tension at which a string is stretched between the bridges is a factor which influences the admission of "partials." Low tension generally yields a flute-like tone,[3] due to the paucity of

---

[3] The early piano did not always give a flute tone, because its low tension string was struck with a very hard and sharp-faced little hammer. A skilful player using and understanding an old instrument can obtain varying tone results. He is aware that a quick blow induces a bright, tinny tone, a gentle touch a mandolin tone, and so on. In old instruments, the touch also governed the recoil of the hammer: in fact, sometimes the touch, of itself, *caused* the rebound of the hammer. The square piano of, say, 1780 had a string tension of about 90 lb. A modern grand has a string tension of possibly 210 lb. (It may be interesting to note that the tension on a violin string runs from 12 lb. to 23 lb.)

harmonics. High-tensioned wires give a nearer approach to trumpet tone,—a blaze of colour.

The modern piano hammer, though soft and rounded at the striking face, undoubtedly increases the tension of a string during the blow. A struck string is increased in tension during the moment of extreme vibration. If a heavy and rapid blow, induced from a sharp and heavy touch, much increases the tension, a fuller and richer tone may be the result, because the vibrations are more complex. The question of the elastic limit of the wire has a part to play in this connection: also the co-efficient of restitution of the hammer felt. Expressing this more simply: If the outer layer of the hammer be soft and curved, the blow will commence gently; then if the under layers of felt are harder, the pressure will increase rapidly to a maximum at a moment when the string and hammer are relatively at rest. As the hammer recoils the pressure dies away. The time-pressure curve may not be symmetrical: the pressure is less during the rebound of the hammer. The immediate point of all this is: Does a variation of touch influence the period of adhesion of hammer and string during both the early and later moments of the blow? If a clinging or lingering touch—some text-books call it a "clawing" touch—delays the recoil of the hammer into check, the hammer momentarily acts as a damper, with an important influence on the ultimate tone.

The writer is under the impression that piano-action makers have always endeavoured to secure a recoil that is irrespective of the blow-power, and thus of the speed of the travel of the hammer. The manner in which the action is set up in the piano is a factor which influences recoil: as also is the angle which the string makes with the hammer as they meet. Some hammers will dither up the string under a powerful blow. The hammer should be not quite rectangular to its shank.

Under a master's hand the perfect piano gives a *steadiness* of tone and an even resonance which may be employed to portray the grandeur of a storm or the limpidity of a running stream.

To bring the human mind close to the heart of all things, to give that pleasure of peace and comfort, the music of the world's masters must use a tone which is full, vital, warm and sympathetic, a tone which is edged with both silver and velvet. Let the piano possess this quality of tone, but also let the tone be even throughout the range and fixed in quality. From gentlest breath and thund'rous roll, the colouring must be the same.

The organ is the instrument for those who strive after colour schemes. But no instrument is so popular as the "orchestra in ordinary" to the household of the poor and the rich. And if suggestions for increasing the potentialities of the piano as a vehicle of musical expression are desired, they will come—in fact, they must come—from other and entirely different directions to that of "touch."

CHAPTER II

Quality of Tone

THE question whether a pianist can vary the tone of his instrument much or little does not affect the all-important fact that the main basic tone must be good. Tone, which is only an accepted expression for quality of sound, may be harsh and hard, biting and brilliant: it may be coarse, dissonant, uneven,—or pure, sweet, full and mellow. Tone can come out of a piano in chunks, or it can be drawn out as smoothly as silk on the weaver's loom. Again, tone can be flat, dull, emotionless, devoid of sparkle: the complete opposite of which is a range of treble notes suggesting nothing so much as the tone of the glockenspiel. Musical tone is ever a matter of individual taste and judgment.

It is, therefore, difficult to lay down any rule for general guidance or acceptance as to what the components of a good tone should be. Certainly it must have sustaining power,—that is to say, it must not be what is known technically as "tight." The strings of a piano must have freedom to sing well. There must be an absence of noise, of other sound, accompanying the notes themselves. There must be no noise from the means of striking the string: no "thud" on the soundboard. The tone must not change between the beginning and ending of its duration.

But of what composition must be the tone itself? That a very definite compound of prime pitch and upper-tone components is necessary is common knowledge. But no one has yet given to the piano manufacturer an ideal composition for the retinue of tone partials. The musical ear recognises quickly a good tone. But it is a difficult thing to analyse tone accurately. True, the actual tone components of an isolated string in its respective intensities can be known by means of a vibration microscope. But to dissect the components of a string when it is one of many, and which is fixed to a soundboard, is practically impossible. The sound produced under such conditions is augmented and modified by sympathetic vibrations from unstruck strings. This co-vibration is set up by the impulses passing up and down the soundboard bridge.

There is one outstanding quality of tone which the pianist desires: it is resonance. Above all things, a pianist likes an instrument which is resonant, and this because resonance gives brilliance and buoyance. It gives command over the eventual tonal effect. When an artist speaks of an instrument being wooden and lifeless, the probability is that the tone is in the strings, but is lost or spoilt by the soundboard. Should, however, the tone of a piano as existing in the struck strings be of poor and unsatisfactory quality, the most perfectly balanced and sensitive soundboard in the world will not improve the nature of the impulses received from the vibrating strings.

It has been said that really high-grade pianos, no matter what their country of origin, compare very favourably with each other in so far as tone *quality* is concerned. Few will dispute this assertion: yet the *possibilities* of a piano is a point often overlooked. And by possibilities is meant the reserve of tone. English and German instruments, generally, carry a fine reserve, especially in the lower range of the compass. The American instrument, on the other hand, seldom yields anything resembling a good quality of tone under heavy playing. The French piano can be mercurial in its qualities: there is a charming and refreshing delicacy elicited by a limpid touch, but it is apt to become painfully "thin." At its best, French tone is exquisitely pellucid and silvery: at its worst, it is hard, tinny and dissonant,—which is only another way of explaining that there is an absence of tone-reserve.

It is to be noted that, during the last fifty years, there has been a considerable development in tone: the tone of the piano of to-day is superior. It is fuller and richer: it is more "vital" than that of the pianos of the middle Victorian period. The reason is not far to seek. With the accumulation of knowledge, a more complete understanding has become general of the complex vibrations which are the basis of beautiful musical tone. The pianos of the 'sixties and 'seventies possessed a very hard-nosed hammer. To-day there is a steel string at a high tension (about 180 lb. to 200 lb.) which is hit by a soft-faced hammer. Improvements in the manufacture of steel wire facilitated the introduction of higher-tension string lengths. The wires could be drawn tighter: which meant that heavier wires (i.e., of larger diameter) had to be employed. To agitate such wires by a *hard* hammer is to get an effect not unlike that produced by striking a metal bar: hence the advent of the soft hammer.

The earlier pianos had a hard tone, a thick tone: yet it was quickly lost. A fault sometimes found in pianos of to-day is the "shallow" tone, with which an artist has to work hard to obtain volume. This type of tone is the result, probably, of a combination of low-tension strings with hammers too soft.

Musicians may be heard to say that a composition is suited only to a certain type of piano. An example was once quoted in two modern pieces. The first portrayed a storm at sea: the pounding of the surf on the rocks: the deep, distant roar. A heavy, sonorous tone was necessary. The second piece was the " Spinning Girls of Carantec," representing a group of women in the old Breton market, chattering and gossiping at their work. Such a scene required a scintillating tone of extreme clarity and delicacy.

Now, there is no doubt that an artist cannot create quality of tone. They may, through excellence of technique, colour an exist-ing quality: here also the pedalling plays an important part. But as the glory of a cavalry call is only faithfully given by the "blaze" and shrill penetration of the trumpet: so is the common "cook house" call more adapted to the bugle. For the hunter is the horn; but the passionate lover chooses the music of the human voice.

So with pianos: different plans of scaling produce different tones, some bright, some mellow. It is reasonable to ask, how-ever, that a piano shall possess an even quality throughout.

The piano of this day is not only in the homes of the rich: pianos of sorts are within the means of all classes. It should be the aim of makers to secure a good quality of tone in all types of the instrument. The tonal structure should include the "satisfying" quality of the wood-wind,— smooth, lasting and filling. Yet the relief of the "strings" is necessary: and the tone to be a real vehicle of musical interpretation needs to be pointed with the brilliant bite of the French horn and trumpet,— to possess that silvered edge.

Piano technicians with vision have for years been telling the industry that even the "cheap" piano can be a real and worthy household orchestra. Tone production is not only craftsmanship and good material: it is the application of a little orderly know-ledge.

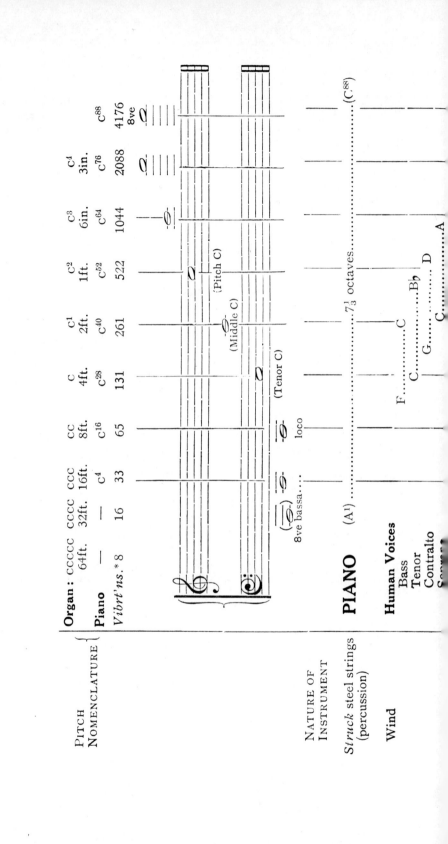

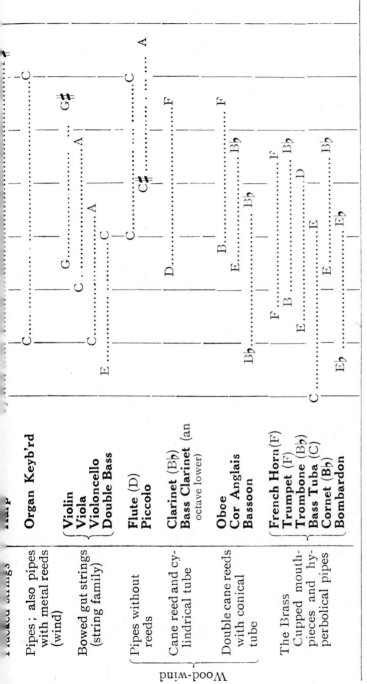

* Per second, approximated to nearest whole number, New Philharmonic standard.

CHAPTER III

Piano Tone compared with the Voice

and other Instruments

THE human voice considered as a musical instrument! The idea is not unfamiliar, yet there is something unusual in the phrase. That the highest place amongst musical instruments must be given to the voice is undoubted. Call to mind the marvellous depth of expression that can be concentrated into a single note: the pathos, the agony that fills one short passage. True, the compass of the voice is limited in one individual: yet, as will be seen from a table which it is intended to produce later, the different varieties taken together give a considerable range, certainly beyond the limits of the staves.

In this chapter, however, we shall compare the piano with the complete field of musical sound-producers, and not only with the voice. It will, therefore, be convenient, before proceeding, to attempt in some form a general category and analysis.

First, the whole range of musical instruments possesses four distinct features. (Fog-horns, sirens and similar sound-producers have precisely the same features.)

(*a*) The vibrating system.
(*b*) The mechanism for exciting the system.
(*c*) The means for amplifying or modifying the sound-energy first produced.
(*d*) The mechanism for producing the scale,— for modulation and for expression.

This is admittedly a wide classification. Sub-analyses immediately suggest themselves. Three examples are worked out to the above group, thus:—

12

THE VIOLIN.

(a) The strings constitute the vibrating system.

(b) The bow, in the hands of the performer, is the exciter.

(c) The bridge; the belly and back, and the air between provide the resonator.

(d) The fingers of the player and the finger-board constitute the scale-producing mechanism.

THE VOICE.[4]

(a) Vocal cords, the ligaments, are the vibrating system.

(b) The breath from the lungs is the exciter.

(c) The resonator consists of the pharynx, mouth and nose; modifying factors are the palate, tonsils, teeth, tongue and lips.

(d) The scale-producing mechanism are the muscles controlling the vocal cords: these muscles have the power to vary the tension and "thickness" of the vocal cords, thus producing notes of different pitches.

THE PIANO.

(a) Cast steel strings provide the vibrating system.

(b) Felted hammers actuated by a train of mechanism called the action and keys are the exciters.

(c) The soundboard bridges and the board itself are the method of amplification.

(d) The piano is a fixed-tone instrument: the scale is fixed by the maker. Variations of "temperament" are only rendered possible by the services of a tuner, who re-fixes the pitch of each note to the new relationship.

---

[4] The outstanding feature of the human voice considered as a musical instrument is that it possesses the unique power of modifying the *quality and degree of sustained sounds*, which makes it possible to distinguish vowels from consonants: in short, the voice gives words as well as music. Consonants are produced by rapid and irregular vibrations; vowels, including those consonants which are scientifically vowels, are given by the favouring of certain partials. If a vowel in a word, say *oo* in *doom*, is sung in different pitches, the tongue and lips are unchanged. The vocal cords alone are varied. The muscles alter the frequency of the chords: thus the vibrating system is changed, but not the means of resonation. If, however, the complete word *doom* is sung in different pitches, then the tongue, lips, &c., have to be set on each occasion. These facts can be verified by experience in a moment.

A brief consideration of the scale-producing mechanism (*d* in the previous groups) of the piano exposes the limited nature of a fixed-tone instrument, such as the piano, organ, clarinet, &c. Modulation is certainly possible within the bounds of the equally-tempered tuning scale. Concordant intervals, by which is meant beatless intervals, cannot be obtained: also the beauty of *portamento* passages is impossible. These may be minor limitations, but it will be generally conceded that a fixed-tone imposes very great restrictions. The voice and instruments of the stringed group, as also a trombone, must conform to the piano.

Proceeding with this comparison of the pianoforte with other musical sound-producers, it is necessary to leave the actual sphere of sound *production* and to examine those characteristics which distinguish one musical instrument from another. A general survey must suffice, and five headings may be tabulated. Illustrations will be added of opposed examples of instruments in each group, because a fuller understanding of the analysis is facilitated thereby.

(1) The quality of sound emitted, known to all as *tone*.
    (*a*) Penetrating: Glockenspiel, Trumpet.
    (*b*) Muffled: French horn, Bass drum.

(2) The compass, the range of notes.
    (*a*) Large: Harp, Piano,[5] 'Cello.
    (*b*) Small: Double bass, Oboe.

(3) The scale: the interval relationship of the notes. The possibilities or restrictions for sounding many or one notes: the facility for melody or harmony.
    (*a*) Harmonic series: Bugle, Cornet.
    Melody.
    (*b*) Chromatic scale: Piano, Organ.
    Harmony.

(4) The power or volume of sound produced as against its delicacy.
    (*a*) Power: Trombone, Bombardon.
    (*b*) Delicacy: A 16ft. dulciana organ stop.

(5) The change of intensity and possible modification of the sound.
    (*a*) Sustained: Violin, Voice, Harmonium.
    (*b*) Evanescent.   Cymbals, Piano, Dulcimer.

[5] Note that the piano has the longest keyboard range of all instruments. Strictly speaking, it has seven and one-third octaves (not seven and a quarter), — i.e., eighty-eight notes. The frequency of the lowest is about 27 complete vibrations per second, and of the highest 4176.

In some of the above instances, there may be much more subtle distinctions to draw. A violin played *pizzicato* passes into another group. The voice, and indeed the piano in some respects, are incapable of belonging to one group alone. These last two because they contain so many features of the complete orchestra.

The earlier examination of tone has shown how quality is dependent upon the strength of a prime pitch and the relative strength of a retinue of partials. Each class of musical instrument has a tonal composition of its own. The majority of instruments possess a tone which contains the full harmonic series. Some contain in their tonal make-up a proportion of enharmonic partials: church bells and gongs come within this group. It will be interesting to recall that bell founders *claim* to be able to eliminate the melancholy effect of the minor third by turning and boring at certain distances in the bell. A bell has five chief tones: the lowest (called the hum-note); the fundamental; the tierce; the quint; and the nominal. The pitch distance between the hum-note and the nominal is two octaves, while the tierce and quint give a major third and fifth in the higher octave.

A Comparison of Compass.

The tabulation given at the beginning of this chapter shows the general nature and range of all the important instruments.

Pianoforte makers, for their own reasons, number the keys of the piano from left to right, A^1 being the lowest bass note and C^{88} the highest treble note. Organ makers adopt a different system for fixing the pitch of a note, as also do singers and other instrumentalists. A comparison is shown of the various methods. It will thus be possible to speak of a note and to locate its position with certainty.

In discussing the compass of certain instruments, it must be remembered that the height or depth of the limiting notes may not always agree with the pitch of the written sign. Again, a trumpet may be in F and E♭ or in B♭ and A♮. The tradition of an individual instrument often determines its compass. The pianoforte, of course, only varies within the range of the absolute pitches,—that is, about three-quarters of a semitone.

Continuing our survey of the piano as compared with the whole field of musical instruments, it has been shown that in the direction of compass, the piano is dominant. The harp and the bowed family have the next largest range. A word must, however, be given to the organ.   The organ keyboard has a range, generally, of five octaves, CC to C^4, although the total command of pitch with the organ is considerably greater than that of the piano.

A 64ft. organ pipe produces a note (CCCCC) having only 9 vibrations, which will shake all the glass in a building.   A $\frac{3}{4}$in. pipe produces a note one octave higher than the last C on a $7\frac{1}{3}$ octave piano, and having a frequency of over 8,350 vibrations per second.   This provides a distance of 10 octaves.   While the eye sees only two octaves, the ear can hear up to twelve octaves: but the extreme ranges are not musically useful.

Helmholtz considered that the lowest note, E, on the German four-stringed double bass [p. 267, Ellis translation] was "the lowest really musical note."   The lowest note of the double bass in Beethoven's "Pastoral" Symphony is a 16ft. C (the first C of the piano keyboard; 33 vs. frequency).

The extension of the piano keyboard to C at the treble end is becoming universal, and is due partly to technical reasons concerning the quality of the notes of the extreme register.   Also, piano-player manufacturers use these three additional notes on the coinciding tracker bar for expression devices.   The block of three sharps in the fullest-compass instrument gives a more complete finish to the keys than does the F♯ and G♯ alone.   It has taken about fifty years for the $7\frac{1}{3}$ range to become popular over the 7 octave (A to A) compass.

Mention might here be made of the effect of pitch upon tone.   Key-colour, though non-existent to the physicist, is real enough to the musician.   Pitch is certainly *one* of the controlling forces over the varied tone qualities resulting from a use of different keys.   Again, the limits of human audition play a further part.   If one person cannot hear a sound above a certain pitch, it may not be unreasonable to assume that the sensation produced in the mind of that person by a normal pitched note is very different to the sensation received by a second person.   The fact that tone is composite both in *pitch* and quality strengthens this contention.

Mr. H. Keatley Moore has explained how, when working with Alexander J. Ellis, it was found that some persons could hear a whole octave above others.   One might hear a grasshopper shrilling, while the other experienced complete silence.   What is the more remarkable is the fact that there is no shading away: once a point is passed there is complete silence to the listener.

The highest pitch audible is somewhere about 40,000 vibra-

tions per second.   The lowest could perhaps be put at about 10
per second, and this is only effective as a series of throbs.

We may now pass on to compare the characteristics of a few
instruments.   The piano, it will be noted, contains in its make-up
a little of the tone quality of nearly every other instrument.   It
is this universality of piano tone which prevents a decay of the
popularity of the instrument : it does not become wearisome. Yet
there are certain tonal features which are missing in the piano.
For example, the keen delicacy of the guitar or mandolin, the soft
thud of the harp, the skirl of a blown instrument, the crisp sweetness of the celesta, the staccato of harmonium percussion, or the
beating tone of an harmonium expression stop.   The muffled-
drum effect possible with the piano is due to the primary fact of
percussion and is a feature which lends itself to vulgarisation.
The sustained sounds of the organ, by contrast, are always lack-
ing in accent.

One of the great failings of the piano is the impossibility of
crescendo on a holding note, in which respect it is inferior to the
organ and all bowed and wind instruments.   Yet the piano atones
in giving complete continuous harmony.

The Violin. — The violin requires much from the player.
Everything is possible on the violin : but the demands are considerable.   Being a bowed instrument, the intensity of sound is
sustained.   A master of its technique can express the emotions
of the human heart with ease.   It is the fact that the whole mechanism of sound production is so much under the control of the
performer that these extraordinary achievements are possible.
Also that the tone, unlike that of the piano and harp, which inevit-
ably dies away, can be sustained.   The piano is like the "moving
finger:" it is impossible to lure back or cancel the energy once
given to a key. The violin bow, however, can cancel any falseness
or imperfection in its next immediate movement.   The piano
resembles the cymbals : its tone dies away, and there is no
modification.

The Voice.—A singer has a command and control of resources
which has no parallel in any instrument made by the hand of
man : the work of nature is supreme.   The resonant piano may
be full of infinite possibilities : it completes the trinity of composer, performer and medium of expression, but how immense
are its failings when compared with the work of Nature ?   The
most perfect tone produced by the mechanism of man cannot
bear comparison with the notes of birds of the air.   The birds of

a tropic jungle have a rippling, liquid fulness and vitality which no instrument can ever hope to yield.

The Harp.—It is strange that the harp finds such small patronage: its tone mingles, yet is never lost in the mass of wood-wind and brass. As distinct from the piano, the tone of the harp is definitely under the control of the player, because the strings can be plucked at various points, also in varying ways. Piano tone is only altered by pounding,—by thumping. (The piano, again, does not offer quite the same facilities for the display of a shapely arm as does the harp!) The harp always produces a thrum quite apart from the musical note.

The Flute.—Here we have one of the simplest instruments both in tone and construction. The paucity of its harmonics produces a unique tone, which can portray sentiments of desolation, humility and resignation better than any other orchestral sound.

> But presently
> A velvet flute note fell down pleasantly
> Upon the bosom of that harmony.
> And sailed and sailed incessantly
> As if a petal from a wild-rose blown
> Had fluttered down upon that pool of tone.

For the expression of certain sentiments, the piano cannot compete with a simple flute tone.

The Piccolo.—Notable for the incisive brightness at an extreme compass. Both the flute and the piccolo are capable of extreme agility, perhaps second only to the piano.

The Clarinet.—"Melting" aptly describes the beauty of clarinet tone. All these instruments are, of course, limited to "melody;" there is an extraordinary sweet fulness in their tone.

> The silence breeds
> A little breeze among the reeds
> That seem to blow by sea marsh weeds,
> Then from the gentle stir and fret
> Sings out the melting clarinet.

The Trombone.—Here is an instrument far removed from the piano, an instrument of great power, rich and heavy of tone, unsuitable for florid movements, yet possessing an exquisite grandeur for slow and legato passages.

The Trumpet.—The piano has yet to be built which will yield anything like the regal clang of the trumpet. Unlike the cornet, the trumpet does not easily lend itself to the ephemeral or the commonplace. Trumpet tone is always brilliant and noble.

Horn Tone.—Piano tone is perhaps the most gratifying of all simple tones, and that because it is so complex. It may be held by some that the horns have a quality equally complex and gratifying as that of the bass notes of the piano. Certainly the lower notes on a horn are exquisitely "full." It is computed that these lower notes have a composite tone made up of 50 per cent. intensity for the prime pitch, and 20 or 30 overtones sharing in diminishing intensity the remaining 50 per cent. of tone volume. No doubt it is this amazing richness of overtones (which is also sometimes found in the bass voice) that can so wonderfully portray the tender sentiments of the poet. Too great a strength of harmonics is unsuitable for the universal tone which must be the ideal for the piano : because the piano is more used as a complete orchestra and not as an orchestral instrument.

Vladimir de Pachmann has expressed the view of the completeness of the piano. His words are worth recording. "When I first commenced the study of music, I was six years old. My father was a violinist. Naturally, he taught me the violin ; and it was not until I was ten years old that he saw that my chief interest was in the piano. Then he started to teach me the piano. The piano is the finest solo instrument in the world: *because it is complete.* It is even more complete than the organ, because its keyboard, its normal expressive range, is greater, although its variety of tone is not as great as that of the organ. I have never liked any other of the solo instruments as such. In the combination of the grand orchestra, they are magnificent : but otherwise they seem incomplete to me."

In concluding this chapter, we would like to quote from a congratulatory address sent by the National Museum of Sweden at Stockholm to the Trustees of the National Gallery on the occasion of the recent centenary celebrations. The address, which was printed in *The Times*, contains some remarkable musical comparisons :—

"Raphael's transparent violin," it says, "sings over the dark pitch of Titian's 'cello, and the emotional notes of Hogarth's deep bassoon are heard through the clear spinet harmonies of Chardin ; above them all, the sound of Rembrandt's tuba, terrifying as the trump of doom, soft as caresses on a feverish brow." The address concludes : "It is our stedfast hope that this prototype, your gallery of art, your wonderful temple of notes may, until the end of time, preserve and express that beauty which has a fresh message for every one and which is bound neither by nationality nor language."

CHAPTER IV

The Forms of the Piano

THE HORIZONTAL.

IT will be appropriate now to pass to a consideration of the varied forms which the modern piano assumes. Free from empiric vagaries, the horizontal grand is a beautiful and noble instrument. It has long taken a definite form, being the final evolution of applied acoustics and craftsmanship: it is a musical sound-producer constructed in an ideal acoustic form. For the production of the best tone, there is nothing to equal the full-sized grand.

The concert grand usually approaches 8ft. in length, though occasionally an instrument just under 9ft. is seen; while Bösen-dorfer of Vienna used to make a grand 10ft. in length. Until a a few years ago a "grand" was almost invariably a good piano, for the form had not been unduly commercialised. A cheap grand was unknown. Such is not the case to-day. Speaking with full appreciation of the high qualities of the "grand" pro-per, it is undeniable that to shorten its length is to take away one of its chief advantages: and this because the length of the string is thereby restricted. It does not necessarily follow that the tone of the very small grands, which are a vogue to-day, is better than that of many high-grade upright pianos, notwithstanding the advantage of horizontal form. The string-length is so short that the flexibility is insufficient, and there is danger that the result-ing tone may be either thick or "barky" and generally poor.

There are many reasons why, for the production of the best piano tone, the horizontal grand of adequate length must always remain supreme. Some of these reasons are fully understood: others are not. Piano technicians of standing are themselves always seeking that knowledge which, when found, will enable them to reproduce the tone of the grand in an upright instrument.

An examination of certain features of grand construction will explain why the tone results of horizontal pianos are usually superior to those of the upright instrument.

The soundboard of the grand is in a better position acoustically. The top of the grand, when raised, has the effect of deflecting the sound somewhat. The tone produced in the horizontal instrument comes away freely from both top and underside of the soundboard. In the upright, it is not unusual for the rear side of the soundboard to back against a wall. Again, the action and general case-work of the upright must have some modifying effect on the tone.

The soundboard of the grand is furnished with a dense continuous rim, which is more complete than that of the upright piano. Impulses arising from the movements of the strings pass freely to the edges of the board, whence they recoil without loss. But probably the greater reason for the finer beauty of grand tone lies in the fact that more length of string may be employed. In this greater length is a less rigid vibration. Complex vibrations can work their own sweet will: hence the greater body and colour of tone resulting. The hammer of the grand is more heavily felted than that of the upright.

The soundboard of any piano is more flexible in the direction of its front face, because the pressure of the strings downwards on the surface of the board restricts freedom of movement in the direction in which they are pressing. Now, the blow of the hammer in the horizontal instrument tends to drive the string *upwards* and *away* from the soundboard. In the upright piano, the string first moves inwards, and thus against a less flexible resonator.

The means of agitating the string by the action of the horizontal grand is decidedly superior. Touch, repetition and damping are all better. Further, the performer has a more complete command over the piano, due mainly to different and important features in grand action construction. When we remember how freely the right-hand pedal is employed, the necessity for perfect damping is at once apparent. The damper of the grand falls by gravity and with a finality quite its own: the damper of the upright action is driven against the string by the release of a spring, a method much less effective and bringing a twang or buzz to the ultimate sound. The checking or damping of tone is next only in importance to the quality of tone first produced, because indifferent silencing is accompanied by noise foreign to all musical sounds. There is a further explanation why the grand damper is so exceedingly and happily efficient: it falls more completely over the most active point of the whole string,— i.e., the strike point. In the nature of things, this cannot ever be accomplished in the upright piano action.

There is, of course, no essential difference in the general *plan* of construction of the concert, the boudoir, or the baby grand. The boudoir instrument and the drawing-room grand run from 5ft. 6in. to 6ft. 6in., while the baby-grand may be not more than, say, 4ft. 6in. in length. The want of harmony and sharpness in the curves of the smaller baby-grand cases give to the whole an appearance little short of grotesque.

THE UPRIGHT.

(A) *The Overstrung*.[6]—The public has been educated, at least of late year, to take the overstrung form for granted. What is there in this method of stringing that will explain this preference? The overstrung piano has three distinct advantages over the straight or vertically strung instrument, and there are no accompanying disadvantages. A string running diagonally across the piano must necessarily be longer than one running parallel to the ends of the case. A longer string, considered with certain other factors, dictates tone improvement. The main advantage of the cross-strung piano, however, is that the bridges are placed more centrally upon the soundboard and further removed from the dead and lifeless edges of the board. The third advantage in overstrung construction is that the bridges are in a better relative position to the soundboard bars. (These bars are, of course, conveyors of tone.) The bass register of an overstrung piano has a further small influence at work in its favour: the bass bridge, owing to the necessity of clearing other strings, is built up high from the board. This is thought to be a form conducive to the best results.

(B) *The Vertical.* — Out of the four countries having well-developed piano industries, England is the only one which continues to make a vertically strung instrument. These pianos are produced in large numbers in this country, and there is little economic reason to suppose that the quantity will fall. The vertical is usually a cheaper type of piano: but there is no reason

---

[6] There is no certain information as to who first introduced cross or over stringing in pianos. A record in the U.S.A. patent office shows that in 1830 Alpheus Babcock took out a patent "for cross stringed pianofortes." When it is remembered, however, that some eighteenth century clavichords were overstrung, the question loses much of its interest.

why it should not be a piano almost as good as the more expensive overstrung. Conditions, mainly economic, confine the straightstrung piano to the cheaper grades. To some degree these conditions prevent the vertical piano from being a true musical instrument, which is a fact always to be deplored. Although there is a large market in all industrial centres for a cheap piano, the more ambitious and renowned firms rarely if ever attempt to compete for any part of it with a vertical. The result is that the small workshop can exist commercially and in relatively large numbers, though at the expense of the musical quality of the instrument, arising from lack of standardisation and of advanced technical knowledge. The poverty of tone of cheap pianos is due more to indifferent organisation and absence of insistent supervision than to unskilled workmen.

(c) *The Oblique.*— This form can be described as "a piano half vertical and half overstrung," and this because its diagonal stringing secures perhaps half the advantages of the overstrung instrument. Early French makers, Erard particularly, made some very beautiful obliques. Though this form finds few supporters in England, French makers continue to build a number, and these pianos are always distinguished for good workmanship and beautiful tone, even though it may be of the French "thin" quality.

THE ART PIANO.

The first art pianos were constructed by early Italian makers. Hans Ruckers of Antwerp had many of his harpsichords decorated by the great Flemish painters. Some of the more famous art pianos are the Broadwood grand built for Sir Alma Tadema; the Bösendorfer grand built for the Empress Elizabeth of Austria; the Steinway at the White House, Washington; and the Rudolf Ibach Sohn jubilee instrument.

The art piano has a very definite place to fill in that it has a real influence upon the design of the commercial piano. There is no reason why the influence of art upon character and taste should not find expression through even the cheapest of pianos.

VARIED TYPES OF MANUFACTURE.

The "aliquot-scaled" piano of Blüthner is one in which an unstruck string is added to the higher treble notes, the object claimed being amplification due to co-vibration. The fourth string is tuned to the pitch of the first harmonic,—i.e., one octave higher than the parent note, but obviously not in the last octave of the range, where it agrees with the prime pitch. It is doubtful whether any considerable volume is added to the note, and it will be accounted to the tuner for righteousness when he tunes these "sympathy strings."[7]

In the duplex-scaled piano, it is stated that that part of the string which does not vibrate (known technically as the dead-string length) is left free to move and thus to amplify the note. It is difficult to see how any extensive help is thus obtained. And even if there is a slight movement in this length of string, which runs between the iron-frame and the soundboard bridge, the result can only be that of adding a general *en*harmonic buzz to the tone. If the vibrating length of a piano string is regulated in its pitch relationship to other notes, it is axiomatic that the dumb part of the same string cannot likewise be adjusted. This because tuning a piano string consists of subtracting or adding tension between the speaking and the dumb lengths. In the normal piano, dumb or dead lengths are "listed" to prevent any possibility of vibration.

Instruments intended for hot climates and for climates changing to complete saturation need a special form of manufacture, though involving no fundamental differences. Veneer cannot be used; all parts must be screwed as well as glued; the felt-work is frequently impregnated with arsenical compounds to prevent attacks of tropic insects. Action feltwork has to be tied and sewn. The coverings of the keys must be pinned.

Dr. Rimbault tells us that at the Exhibition of 1851 there was "a fiddle piano, wherein a violin, connected by mechanism with a second row of keys, played a dismal unison with the right hand of the performer." The piano with additional pedals offers un-limited scope to the unmusical craftsman. Metal discs by means of a pedal are interposed between the hammers and strings.

The transposing piano is frequently placed before the music-ally innocent. Sometimes the keyboard moves or the action shifts laterally. In other arrangements the keys are divided in their length, so that each length moves independently: therefore, the front length of, say, key C can be moved to operate the back length of, say, key C♯, D, or B. Sebastian Erard, it is recorded,

---

[7] Aliquot scaling, though perhaps not very effective in practice (it is only applied to the extreme treble), is nevertheless in accordance with the proper application of natural laws of acoustics. When the soft pedal of a grand is in operation, the whole of the instrument is immediately converted into what is the same as the aliquot scaling. The duplex-scaled piano, however is on a very different footing.

constructed a piano with a sliding keyboard for Marie Antoinette, Queen of France, who had a voice of limited compass. In similar cases, a transposing piano may have some use.

The piano with pedal attachment is occasionally used by organ students. Combination piano-and-reed organ instruments have often been patented and made: the reeds are introduced beneath the keybottom. The little portable piano, which can be carried from room to room and placed upon a table, is a type representing considerable skill in design. The piano-organ of the London streets is, of course, only a sort of piano carried on a crank-axle truck: it has a "tune-barrel," the hammers are usually covered with leather, and a tremolo attachment is added; there are no dampers.

The penny-in-the-slot electric piano is, so far as general construction is concerned, an ordinary piano with an automatic operating-attachment: sometimes drum and other orchestral effects are added. The Continental café or a "down town" hal of a Middle West town, is the natural sphere of these electrical contraptions, though some are found nearer home.

The tuning-fork piano has a restricted compass. A down-striking hammer (exactly similar to a piano-action hammer) strikes a tuning fork and rebounds. The lower bass forks have a somewhat unpleasant tone quality, but the treble has a distinctly sweet, bright yet delicate tone. It mingles well in the small orchestra. Scientifically, the tuning-fork piano is interesting, because as a musical instrument it forms a class apart. It is an instrument without any upper partials, — i.e., harmonics. This piano never requires tuning; if it did, it would be impossible to fine tune the forks without recourse to a portable series of twelve chromatics: unless a tuner were found who could tune by a sense of pitch-distance alone.

The celesta is a substitution of the glockenspiel, and seems to have become popular, though the cloying sweetness of its tone demands sparing a use. It is a percussion instrument and possesses a train of mechanism not unlike a piano-action. The vibrating system is tuned steel bars, to which dampers are attached: the keyboard is chromatic, with twenty-five or thirty-seven notes.

The Virgil practice clavier may be mentioned. It consists of a $7\frac{1}{3}$-octave keyboard which is dumb. By means of regulating screws, the weight of touch can be varied from 2 oz. to about 8 oz. Also the "click" accompanying the use of a key can be varied from the depression to the release of the finger pressure.

CHAPTER V

The Pedals

A PERFECT musical instrument must, it is to be supposed, possess among other things a complete command over all varieties of colour and colour graduation. After the human voice—which, of course, possesses these qualities in a unique degree—the piano has very strong claims. It is, however, the pedals, and principally the sustaining pedal, which bestow upon the piano the quality of colour variation.

It would be a mistake to imagine that the function of the "loud" pedal is merely to sustain sounds, while the fingers are engaged elsewhere. The right pedal is a reinforcing pedal. True, it also sustains sounds; but it has another function, perhaps incompletely understood,—that of producing colour variations. It is, in effect, a re-arranger of overtones. The performer is aware, consciously or unconsciously, that the sustaining pedal alters the tonal composition of a note, and thus adds extensively to the material at his disposal. This means of reinforcement and re-arrangement of tonal results is ever at the instant use of the artist.

Thus it is to be seen that pedals are no mere appendage to a piano. Modern music demands great skill and subtlety in their use. The composer has come to regard the pedals as an integral part of the instrument. A brief enquiry, therefore, into their origin and development would seem not to be inappropriate.

The harpsichord possessed "stops," and these were copied by the early makers of pianos. These stops were pedals in every way except that they were not always operated by the feet. There was a forte or damper-lifting stop: a soft stop and a buff stop, the latter interposing soft cloth or leather between the jacks and the strings. There was also the lute stop.

The early horizontal piano had the forte or damper-lifting pedal, also, at a later date, a soft pedal which moved the keyboard and action bodily to the right. In the early cabinet or upright instrument, when the soft pedal was depressed, it was usually the action only which moved: the keys were stationary. The una corda of Beethoven was a double shift: a hand-stop on the keyblock enabled the hammers to strike one string only. Two strings were struck when the pedal was in use, and in the normal course the three strings were struck by the small leather-faced hammers of that day.

Returning to the modern instrument:

The Pedals of the Grand.

The horizontal piano of to-day always has, of course, the forte pedal. It may be remarked that its name, "forte," is not well chosen, for this pedal is equally employed in *pianissimo* passages. It could more accurately be named the damper-lifting pedal. The faculty of having all strings undamped enables the marvellously wealthy field of sympathetic vibration to be tapped at will. A complete mastery of the right pedal demands a quick ear and a fine sensibility. This pedal must be released instantly when confusion due to dissonances of overtones is threatened. Yet it widens considerably the artist's bounds of expression. Perhaps the remarkable command of colour gradation which the damper-pedal bestows will explain, in part at any rate, the claims of musicians to be able to vary the quality of tone by touch. Also, it may be observed here that the soft pedal of the grand is something very much more than the means of reducing the volume of tone. Is it not possible that the extraordinary facility for animation which the pedals jointly confer is the explanation of the failure of pianists to distinguish between pedal and touch effects?

The soft pedal of the horizontal piano has an influence over the ultimate tone composition of a combination of notes no less important than that of the right pedal. The mechanism of the grand soft pedal seems to stand the test of time. Its sliding action and keyboard is still maintained, though a few grands are now made wherein the softened effect is obtained by damping one or two strings. The sliding clavier method has certain distinct objections. There is a heavy pedal action; there are mechanical disadvantages resulting in uneven hammer and action wear; noises easily develop; the keyboard moves under the hand of the performer. Withal, it holds its own, and not without reason. The unstruck string of each note — two only being struck when the pedal is down—vibrates sympathetically. It so vibrates because it is undamped, and is free to respond to the movements imparted by its sisters to the soundboard bridge upon which all three are rigidly held. That a distinct and pleasing quality of tone is obtained is not open to doubt: further there is an added charm in the reduced volume due to fewer strings being struck. The ideal soft pedal yields a tone "like softest music to attending ears."

There is an additional point concerning the soft pedal of the grand type of piano which demands notice. The soft effect cannot be graduated: it is all or nothing. With a sliding action, a hammer must hit either two or three strings. Further, unless the indentations of the steel wire in the hammer faces are exactly opposite the strings, a buzzing and snarling quality of tone is the result. The reason is that the edges of the cuts in the felt act as a partial damper to the vibrations. Thus the soft pedal of the horizontal piano must always be fully and firmly depressed and released. There are a few grands (mostly Austrian) to be found where a third pedal is added; this additional pedal interposing a strip of felt between the hammer and strings. It is unwise to attempt graduations with this device unless there is a graduated thickness in the *depth* of the felt strip. The strips are always graduated in their length, or should be, between bass and treble.

A word must be given to a form of soft pedal which is unique. When depressed, this left-hand pedal mutes two strings of each note by wedging firmly a thick felt pad or damper between them. It is not a very satisfactory way of reducing the volume of sound from an instrument.

The tone-sustaining pedal (rarely to be found in Europe) can be applied equally to the upright and to the grand piano, but it is seldom fixed to the former. This pedal, sometimes called the sostenuto, is a selective damper-sustaining device: its chief features will be discussed later. It is strange that its development and use should have been left to American piano manufacturers and musicians.

THE PEDALS OF THE UPRIGHT.

In discussing the two pedals of the upright instrument, it will be well to commence with a word concerning the *upright action*, because it would be quite correct to regard the pedals as extensions of the action levers. The sticker action having been superseded some thirty years ago in all grades of pianos, the sliding action—to be operated by the left pedal, was abandoned.[8] The deficiency was overcome in two ways: by the céleste, which is a felt strip introduced at will between the hammer and string; and by the reduction in the path traversed by the hammer, when it is called the half-blow. The overdamper upright action was more popular twenty years ago than it is to-day. The underdamper is the one which can be taken for our purpose here.

It is worthy of note that about the years 1890-1910 certain German piano-action makers designed many ingenious actions of the *overdamper* type, some of which embodied a half-blow device, while others were capable of being moved laterally. It would be almost impossible to design an *under*-damper action which would move laterally, unless the damper arms are provided with a fixing which is independent of the action beam. For those who are unacquainted with the essential difference between these two actions, it is well to explain that in the overdamper, like the obsolete sticker, the dampers are *over* or above the point where the hammer meets the string, and these dampers are operated by wires which admit of a certain latitude in regulation and movement. All these features are reversed in the English *under*-damper actions, in which there can be no lateral movement.

Erards have often used an underdamper action which permits of lateral movement: but the rail which carries the dampers is held by the action standards, and is thus independent of the shifting beam.

The soft pedal in the cheaper upright instrument is confined to the céleste strip. In medium and high grade pianos, the restricted striking distance of the hammer is the plan adopted. The céleste is cheap and effective, and enables an action of simpler construction to be used. Its disadvantages are that the felt strip wears and that it alters somewhat the tone quality. The half-blow is scientifically more perfect in so far as the movement of the hammer is concerned: it *is* capable of graduation. If the blow or path of the hammer is two inches (5 cm. is the standard figure), the regulation is such that extreme depression of the soft pedal reduces this to one inch. But a slight depression of the

---

[8] Occasionally an upright piano is to be found in which the keyboard and its check action move bodily, as in a grand. No doubt this type would have been manufactured more extensively were it not for the universal adoption of the overstrung scaling. There are no real difficulties in designing an upright sliding keyboard and overdamper action for a straight-strung piano. When the strings are crossed, however, the difficulties of designing suitably fixed dampers are considerable.

pedal will only slightly reduce the course of the hammer. It will be self-evident, however, that if a rail moves all the hammers forward,[9] there is a space left between the jacks of the action and the notches of the butts. In certain American-made actions this space (technically known as "lost motion" which, of course, it is) is transferred by a repetition-arm or a tight tape to a point where the key meets the heel of the action jack-lever. To perfect the arrangement of reducing the blow, the keys at their front end should drop to the same relative degree that the hammer moves forward. Custom rules that the touch-depth shall be constant. This is not surprising. Nevertheless, the feeling of looseness when the soft pedal is down is objectionable. The key goes down a little before it meets resistance. Hence the superiority of the touch of the horizontal piano.

In Europe, half-blow grand actions are unpopular. In America, they are used, and moreover American makers employ the devices which prevent this lost motion in half-blow actions, both of the grand and upright variety.

The forte pedal of the upright needs no discussion. The only difference between it and its counterpart in the grand is that it does not extend so far up the range in the upright straight-piano. In the upright player-piano, it is carried a few notes higher. This is found necessary, due presumably to the greater number of notes which can be struck at once in the player piano: there is a corresponding increase in the vibration of the soundboard. Undampered notes—say, from C^{64} to C^{76}—are apt to "sing" when they are not required.

The practice pedal, which consists of an unusually thick céleste, needs no explanation. It is useful for the schoolroom; and neighbours of professional pianists may wish that the stop were more widely adopted. The "silencing" stop usually destroys the touch, though it need not do so.

No attention need be given to the hundred and one pedal effects which enthusiastic amateur makers of pianos would add to the instrument. A harpsichord effect, if it is *delicate* in quality, may be useful for the smaller concert-hall. (As a matter of interest, it may be remarked that the harpsichord did not possess a delicate quality of tone: it was harsh, raw and stringy. It was the clavichord, an entirely different instrument, which possessed a

---

[9] Manufacturers of self-playing pianos sometimes divide the half-blow rail into two sections, so that one lockboard lever will soften the bass, and the other the treble: a melody may be accentuated by softening the bass. This arrangement is a trifle crude, and found mostly in cheaper player models.

sweet old-world character. And it was the clavichord upon which the effect called *Bebung* was possible : this vibrato was impossible on any other keyed instrument.)

THE MIDDLE PEDAL.

Musicians in this country have often spoken of the tone-sustaining pedal of the piano as being of doubtful value. Many regard the third pedal as a positive danger, because it is apt to restrict the use of the damper pedal and cause the playing to be dry and patchy. Others dislike it because, as they claim, it tends to complicate the instrument.

To sustain continually only one or two notes by the sostenuto[10] attachment is certainly apt to give a thin tone : but the fact that this pedal has a definite value, even if only by contrast, can scarcely be doubted. The extent to which this additional pedal is in disfavour can be estimated by the statement that only one really high grade piano manufacturer (Steinway) continues to use it. Probably no French maker now employs the device, while very few German pianos are found so fitted. Yet in the United States and in Canada the sostenuto attachment in the form of a third pedal is a recognised adjunct to the first-class instrument.

There is an interesting paragraph in Grove's Dictionary concerning the third, or middle, pedal, but we prefer the concise explanation with which Hipkins dismisses the subject. The "tone-sustaining pedal gives a power of using selected notes undamped." From this it will be seen that it is a disposition of the dampers of the piano action whereby the player may prolong any or many notes by depressing the third pedal. The method of maintaining the dampers off the string is by a thin and finely regulated brass rod; this rod moves sufficiently to catch the damper arms that are "up" at the very moment the pedal is used. Thus to catch and sustain a note, or a group, the foot must depress the pedal directly after the keys are struck, and before they are released. As the whole object is selective, those notes struck *after* the third pedal is down do not continue to vibrate, unless, of course, it so happens that the main damper-lifting pedal is also in use.

It will be realised that the two sustaining pedals can be employed together. The reason why a note, which is struck after the

[10] The best description of the sostenuto pedal ("sostenente") is that it is a selective note-sustaining device. The *pédale de prolongement*, the invention (according to Grove's Dictionary) of a blind Parisian pianoforte maker, was an individual tone-sustaining pedal, and was probably the earliest use of a pedal of this nature. This *pédale de prolongement* was exhibited in 1862.

sostenuto pedal is down, does not continue to vibrate when the player's finger releases the key, is because the catching rod is regulated so that only those dampers which are actually free from the strings at the identical moment that the pedal is depressed are caught.   Subsequent movements of other keys and dampers proceed as usual.

In point of fact, this tone-sustaining pedal is valuable in various ways.   It can prevent the blurring of melody notes; it can catch the lower note of an extended skip; a foundation note of an arpeggio chord can be maintained through rapid changes in the ordinary damper pedal.   Whole chords can be caught and sustained by both the ordinary loud pedal and also by the middle pedal.   A sudden release of the right-hand pedal in these cases creates a distinctive orchestral colouring.   It sometimes happens that the percussive contact of dampers and vibrating strings is undesirable.   To obtain a non-percussive contact, the ordinary damper pedal must be allowed to come up quite gently and slowly, or the middle pedal only employed.

Half-damping (often faultily named half-pedalling) is made supremely easy by the addition of the sostenuto attachment. The effect given by half-damping is occasionally met with : when a bass note is required to be prolonged against moving harmonies above it.   This effect is not always possible, but is available provided the bass note is sufficiently low in pitch to have strongly vibrating strings, and also provided the harmonies take the form of lightly sounded notes well removed in pitch from the bass.   It would seem that there is a recognition of a defect in piano-action design; use is made of the failure to damp immediately both the heavy covered bass strings and the light treble steel strings.

The dampers in the upright piano are markedly inefficient in the damping of the flexible and heavily covered strings.   It is impossible to quench readily a long flexible string which may be six or seven millimetres in diametre : but a mere touch of the damper felt will silence a few inches of thin treble wire.

The sostenuto attachment can be fitted to both horizontal and upright instruments.   In the grand piano, the performer normally has a greater command over the rise and fall of individual dampers, because the damper-arm is controlled directly by the key itself.   In the upright piano, repetition is poorer and damping less effective : it cannot be otherwise.   Damping even in the best and most expensive upright is far from perfect : the damper, instead of falling by gravity, is forced against the strings by small brass springs, and the damper-arm is not under the immediate control of the key.

Yet the third pedal adds to the resources of both forms of the piano. In the upright, it deserves to be particularly welcomed, because this type of piano must, in many ways, be inferior to the horizontal grand. And the inferiority of the upright is nowhere so marked as in the pedal resources, for even the soft pedal is on a very different footing to the combination of reduced volume and the sympathetic effect of co-vibration, as found in the grand piano.

The example below shows the use of the middle pedal in holding a single tone:—

BEETHOVEN
Adagio Op. 31, No. 2

CHAPTER VI

Construction

THE PIANO IN THE BEGINNING.

THE interior economy of the piano is usually called the "scaling." The scale designer has to place at the service of the performer eighty-eight notes : each note must be of pleasing quality, of sufficient strength, and of the correct pitch, the range being over seven octaves. The "scale" of a piano is the succession and the co-relation of measurements which govern the size, shape, and the internal lay-out of the instrument.

The beginning of all things to the piano scale designer is a blank sheet of drawing-paper. If an explanation is attempted of the method of drawing—or better expressed, of "designing"—a scale, an ampler appreciation of the art of piano construction must needs ensue.

Piano scale-designing is an exact example of applied physics. The designer must have a leaning towards mathematics, and considerable draughtsmanship ability is necessary. These qualities, together with a ripe knowledge of the branch of natural philosophy known as acoustics, are all pre-requisites. This because the art of piano construction is the art of combining exact scientific knowledge with an instinct for practical craftsmanship. The work of designing the iron frame, which is really an engineering problem, is a heavy addition. The total stress on a piano frame can easily exceed twenty tons, which, however, due to the overstringing of the wires, is not a direct pull. It is only the few great piano manufacturing houses of the world which design their own frames. The majority of piano scales are modified and adapted to a standard or existing frame.

Certain factors are at the disposal of the scale designer. Every schoolboy knows that a wire, when doubled in length, yields the octave of the first note. Endeavour is made to work as closely as constructional considerations permit to these simple laws of nature. The variable factors in the production of the eighty-eight notes of the piano number four:—

1. The *length* of the vibrating or speaking part of the string.
2. The *tension* to which this active part of the wire is subjected.
3. The *diameter* of the wire employed: that is, the *mass* of wire to be set into vibration.
4. The *density* of the wire employed.

Pitch is determined by the length, tension and weight of the wire string. The greater the tension, the higher the pitch; the greater the length, the lower the pitch; the greater the weight of wire, the lower the pitch.

For ease and facility in calculating the tension of any piano string, the formula given below is very useful, and by using a slide rule the operation is much simplified. The original formula may be stated thus:—

$$n = \frac{1}{2r\,l} \sqrt{\frac{F}{\pi D}}$$

n is the number of vibrations per second (frequency), *2r* the diameter of the string in centimetres, *l* its length in centimetres, F the stretching force on the string, measured in dynes, and D the density of the material of which the string is made in grammes per c.c.

Manipulating: by converting the dynes to pounds, substituting 3·1416 for π, 7·8 for D, and by allowing 2·38 per cent. reduction due to the rigidity effect of the strings as commonly used, there results:—

$$F \text{ (in lbs.)} = \frac{(2r\,ln)^2}{18600}$$

$$\text{or, Tension} = \frac{(\text{Diameter} \times \text{Length} \times \text{Frequency})^2}{18600}$$

Taking an example: Note A♯⁵⁰, 465 frequency,

38·16 centimetres length, 17 gauge = ·975 millimetre, diameter.

$$\frac{(\,·0975 \times 38·16 \times 465\,)^2}{18600} = 160 \text{ lb. tension.}$$

(Early examples of piano work are interesting to present-day manufacturers because the early craftsmen possessed very little scientific knowledge.)

The varying elements at the disposal of the scale designer are bent to yield, not only pitch, but tone quality and tone volume. Other factors have to be observed, such as the resistance of the strings to the hammer blow, the flexibility of the wires, the dimensions of the instrument.

THE SCALE.

An examination of any piano will show that the set-out of the construction falls into, say, three clearly arranged divisions. These are:—

> *The Wrest Plank Scale.*
> *The Bridge Scales.*
> *The Hitch Pin Scale.*

Every detail of piano construction is hinged upon the lay-out of these scales. And these scales in turn are based upon the strike point of each string, or *The Strike Scale.* The first line of a scale drawing is the strike line (E in Fig. 2, Fig. 3, and Fig. 9). This representing the point where the hammer-face meets the string.

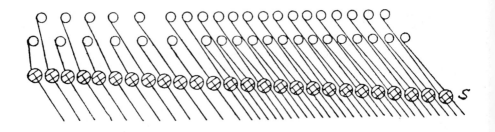

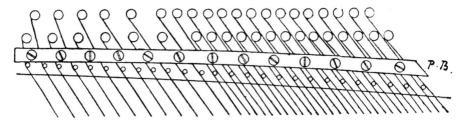

Figure 1

The strike line (which runs horizontally across the face of the strings) is the piano maker's datum. The spacing of the strings along this line represents the string scale, or the width of each note *at the strike point*. The string scale coincides with the hammers, and so the action-butt alignment. The key-pilot scale is the placement of the far end of the keys, and, as is obvious, agrees exactly with the set-out of the action sections. The splay of the keys, and thus the alignment of the front key scale is, to a large extent, independent of the action and pilot scales.

Figure 1 shows two examples of bass wrest-plank scales: one with studs or agraffes (S) and the second with a pressure-bar (PB). In the former, the stud determines the speaking length of the wire, and also creates the necessary side and backward angles (or "rakes"). In the latter, the bar gives the "bearing," and the side-draught is created by the string passing round pins driven into the iron frame.

Figure 2 illustrates the bass-section of a scale drawing for a grand, and shows the upper bridge scales.

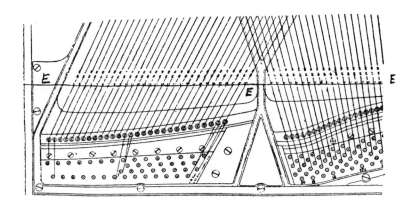

Figure 2

Bass section of wrest plank and upper bridge scales for a horizontal piano.

An illustration of the extreme treble of an upright $7\frac{1}{3}$ octave overstrung scale is shown in Fig. 3, in which E is the strike point; A indicating the frame; B the wrest-pin scale; C the sound-board bridge scale; and D the hitch-pin line.

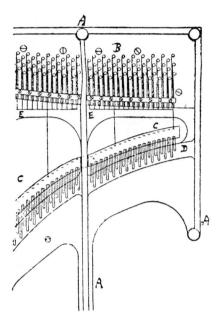

Figure 3
Treble section of 7⅓ octave scale for upright overstrung piano.

A part of the hitch-pin scale of a 7-octave vertical piano is given in Fig. 4: A indicating the soundboard bridge and B the method of hitching to the iron frame.

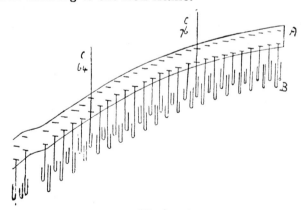

Figure 4
Treble section of hitch pin scale for a vertically strung piano.

THE WIRES.

The essential basis of the modern piano is cast-steel wire of great tensile strength. Step by step, piano tone has advanced with the improvement in the drawing of steel wire. Piano wire is the aristocrat of all steel wires. The finest wire now generally used on the piano measures in millimetres 0·8 diameter: or, in simpler words, it is one-thirtieth of an inch thick. From this size, the increase is fairly regular up to 1·1 mm. diameter. The first thirty notes of the keyboard — that is, the bass strings — are steel cores covered with a copper loading, which loading acts as compensation for the necessary loss of length. The total diameter of bass strings runs from 1·1 mm. to 7·5 mm.: or, roughly, from one twenty-third of an inch to one third of an inch.

Now, in all, there are about 224 strings on a piano: say, 180 trichord, 32 bichord, and 12 singles. Each string is stretched or tensioned over the soundboard at a pull of, say, 200 pounds. One end of a piece of wire is fixed to a hitch pin on the iron frame of the piano: the other end is twisted round a pin which is fixed securely into a wood block. This pin is turned and turned until the wire is at the required pitch. The statement that the piano is a box of stretched strings is, therefore, fairly close to the truth.

The demand for a tone which is clear, full and round, which has volume and which can be sustained, has only been met by the use of perfectly circular wire, this wire being capable of withstanding a strain of over 200 pounds. The crashing chord of the modern virtuoso is due, in the first place, to the provision by the mills of this steel thread, possibly only one-thirtieth of an inch thick, absolutely regular in its length, perfectly circular, and of enormous strength. Be it noted that the breaking strain of good piano wire is over 150 tons per square inch.

The use of wire at high tension has entailed the construction of piano framework capable of withstanding very considerable stress. The art of piano construction might be divided thus:—

1. The design of a wooden stress-resisting structure of an agreed size and shape carrying an iron frame: this structure must be capable of external decoration and must provide accommodation for the keyboard and action.

2. The design of the scale of the instrument.

3. The design and adjustment of keyboard and action: the provision of the means of agitating the original vibrators of the instrument.

4. The provision and fixing of a soundboard, known in the trade as "bellying." This constitutes the means of sustaining and amplifying the sound.

Item (1) needs little explanation here. Items (3) and (4) have been discussed in other chapters. It is the design of the scale which now engages our attention.

SCALE DESIGN.

Figure 5 shows at a glance certain essential features of piano construction. A indicates the top back (or dead) string; B the speaking length; and C the bottom dead string. Examining the drawing,

1. Indicates the wrest plank
2. Corbel of iron frame
2. Upper lip of frame
3. Wrest pin
4. Capo d'astro bar: this determining the limit of the active length of the strings
5. String
6. Laminated bridge, with capping
7. Hitch pin
8. Iron frame
9. Fixing screw
10. Hardwood fillet
12. Soundboard

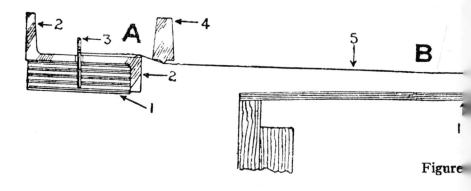

Figure

All pianos, irrespective of their period, and irrespective of their country of origin or of their maker, possess the essential features given in the drawing. These constructive details are constant, whether the instrument is in the horizontal form or whether it is stood up vertically, as in the upright. The outstanding difference between the grand proper and the upright piano is not in the construction of the piano-back (or harp), but in the means of exciting the strings.

The hammer of the grand drives the string upward and away from the soundboard. The hammer of the upright drives the string *inwards* and towards the soundboard.

It is proposed that an examination be made of a scale-design for a boudoir horizontal piano,—that is, a grand of about 5ft. 8in. long. The first restriction is, therefore, one of length. Next, the finished instrument must possess a harmony of outline. Practical considerations dictate that no rim should, at any part of the curve, be on a smaller radius than 4in., measured from the inner surface. The ease of bending is, of course, proportional to the softness of the curves: but the bending of rims for grand pianos requires expensive appliances and highly skilled workmen.

The demand to-day is for an instrument that is capable of very sensitive and effective damping, which demand taxes considerably the ingenuity of the designer, as, at the point where the strings cross,[11] there is very little room for the dampers to work. An equality in tone throughout the range is also demanded. An equal tension scale is one in which each string is subjected to the same pull. This condition favours an even tone, and means also an equal adhesion of strings to the soundboard bridge. It follows that, if one string exerts a greater downward pressure on the

[11] All modern horizontal instruments are overstrung. The chief advantage of overstringing in the larger grands is that the bass bridge is placed in a more responsive part of the soundboard.

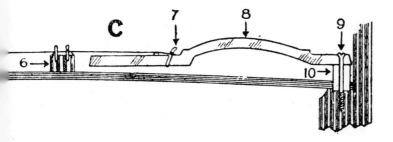

bridge, due to its being at a higher tension, the strings immediately contiguous are less sensitive to the impulses of the moving wire.

The scale when embodied in a piano must, of course, be commercially practicable.

SCALE FOR GRAND OF (SAY) 172 CM. IN LENGTH.

The Strike Scale (see Fig. 8).—This is horizontal, but both the upper and soundboard bridges so conform that the strings are struck at varying proportions of their lengths throughout the compass. In the bass, the string is struck at one-eighth of its length from the upper limit; in the treble, the strike proportion is possibly one-fourteenth. It is generally accepted that, if a node which represents an enharmonic and dissonant tone-partial be made the point of extreme agitation, that partial will be less conspicuous than if the string were struck elsewhere. For this reason and also for the fact that a short string must be struck at a very resisting point near the upper bridge, the strike-proportion is a potent factor in tone production. If the treble strings are struck too low, the thud of impact is returned by the soundboard.

An irregular blow line has never been attempted in piano making, thus the strike-scale is always horizontal. (The harpsichord, it will be remembered, had a row of jacks operated by the "lute" stop, which gave a delicate reedy tone due to the strings being plucked very close to the bridge.)

SCALE ROD. *(See Figure 9).*

The use of a scale rod facilitates the preparation of the drawing: the rod is also the permanent record for a scale design. Paper shrinks, but the shrinkage in a 5ft. length of $\frac{3}{4}$in. by $\frac{3}{4}$in. maple is negligible. Each face of the rod is separately marked, and a datum squared round. This datum can be the inside of the rim, or a central line, but in the example given it is the strike-point of the longest bass string, note A^1.

Face *A* of rod carries the strike scale or spacing
  ,, *B* ,, bottom scale for the steels
  ,, *C* ,, bottom scale for the bass strings
  ,, *D* ,, string lengths

FACE A OF ROD: STRIKE LINE SCALE.

Emphasis must be laid on the fact that the strike scale is the datum from which the whole lay-out and construction of the piano is subsequently determined. The strike-line is, of course,

an invisible line in the finished instrument, except that it can be
visualised in the faces of the hammers throughout the compass.

The spacing of the strings along the strike line is marked on
Face A, the centres on each note being indicated by lines down the
face.   It is preferable to use a geometric method for marking the
strike spacing, as to set-out a scale by successive measurements is
tedious and discouraging.   A "fan" is prepared after the following fashion.   A sheet of paper about four feet square is taken,
and from a base line two perpendiculars (A B) are erected.   A is
divided into (say, 35) 1¼in. spaces, while the lower part of B is
divided into thirty-five ½in. spaces.   See Fig. 6.

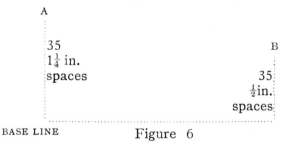

Figure 6

The necessary uniting lines between the two markings are filled
in: the result being as shown in Fig. 7.

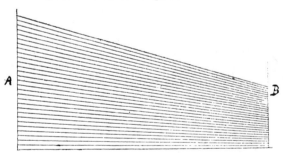

Figure. 7

It is obvious that at any point between the perpendiculars, the
centres of the notes for an *evenly spaced* strike scale can be found.
(It is sometimes necessary to increase slightly the width of the
note space in the lower steels, as the increasing slant of the strings
necessitates more room being given for the hammers and for the
wrest-pin scale.) The ends of each section of strings is first marked
on the rod. Then (with the rod rectangular to the base line of the
fan) the position is found where the correct number of strings

coincides with the same number of lines. The centre of each string position is now pricked off on the rod with a needle, and then squared down with a pencil. Care is necessary to avoid counting spaces for notes.

The strike divisions for the grand scale under examination are given in Figure 8.

To give an equality of width to the strings of each trichord note *at the hammer line*, it is necessary to vary the width of the notes at the top bridge. The graduation may run from 5·5 mm. up to 7 mm. at the extreme treble. A stud upper bearing prevents this graduation, as studs are of a uniform width. The width of the striking face of a piano hammer is generally about 1 cm., and the outer strings of a trichord note should not be less than 1·5 or 2 mm. from the outside edge of the hammer face as the hammer meets the string.

Figure 8 : Strike Line Scale
All measurements are in centimetres.
Ratio of inches to cm. = 26 : 66.   1 inch = 2·54 cm.

Total length of strike scale 123·6 cm., this being from the centre of note A^1 to the centre of note C^{88}.

88 notes : 59 steels, trichord.

29 covered, being 21 bichord and 8 singles.

In all 227 strings.

Bass section .... 25 notes, A^1 to A^{25}

1st section of steels .... 21 notes, $A\sharp^{26}$ to $F\sharp^{46}$
(includes 4 bichord notes, $A\sharp^{26}$ to $C\sharp^{29}$, with covered strings)

2nd section of steels .... 21 notes, G^{47} to $D\sharp^{67}$

3rd section of steels .... 21 notes, E^{68} to C^{88}

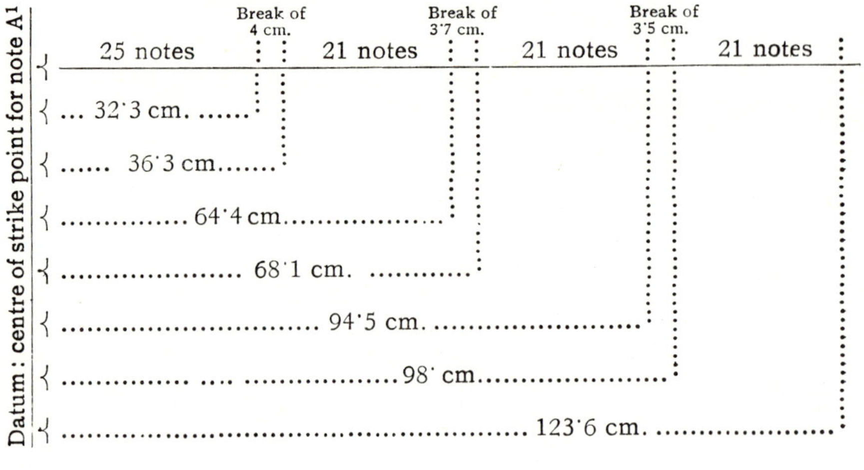

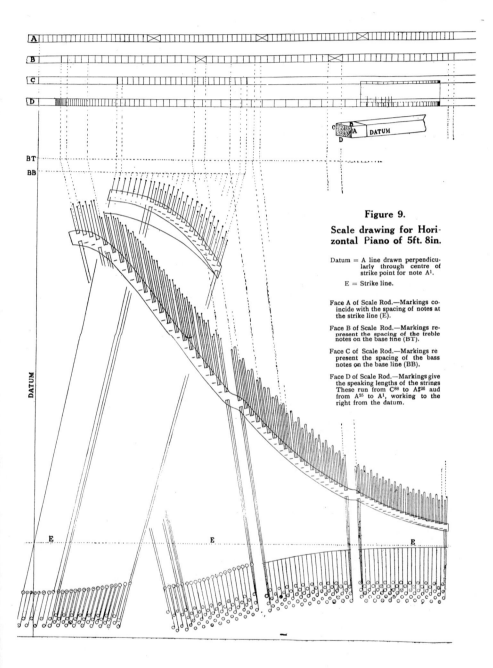

Figure 9.

Scale drawing for Horizontal Piano of 5ft. 8in.

Datum = A line drawn perpendicularly through centre of strike point for note A^1.

E = Strike line.

Face A of Scale Rod.—Markings coincide with the spacing of notes at the strike line (E).

Face B of Scale Rod.—Markings represent the spacing of the treble notes on the base line (BT).

Face C of Scale Rod.—Markings represent the spacing of the bass notes on the base line (BB).

Face D of Scale Rod.—Markings give the speaking lengths of the strings These run from C^{88} to $A\sharp^{26}$ and from A^{25} to A^1, working to the right from the datum.

FACES B AND C OF ROD: BOTTOM SCALES.

The two "bottom-scale lines" are shown in Figure 9. B T is the treble scale line, and B B the bass line. These bottom scale lines are important in that they form a base upon which the centres of notes may be marked. The spacing of the notes along these base-lines governs the fanning of the strings: a single line being drawn for each *note* from the appropriate wrest-pin coil position to the marking B T and B B.

In this particular scale B T is 113 cm. distant from the strike and B B is 109 cm. distant. The details of the spacing of the strings are shown in Figure 10.

It will be seen that the spacing of the bottom scale will govern the distance which the strings of individual notes are apart from each other on the soundboard bridge.

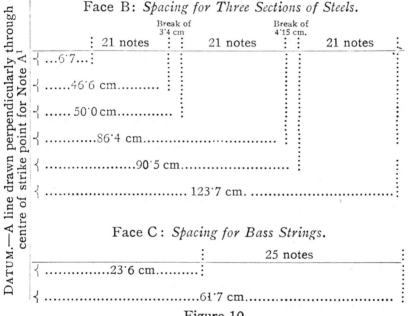

Face B: *Spacing for Three Sections of Steels.*

DATUM.—A line drawn perpendicularly through centre of strike point for Note A¹

Break of 3˙4 cm   Break of 4˙15 cm.

21 notes   21 notes   21 notes

...6˙7...
......46˙6 cm..........
...... 50˙0 cm..............
...........86˙4 cm.........................
...................90˙5 cm.......................
.... 123˙7 cm. ....

Face C: *Spacing for Bass Strings.*

25 notes

...............23˙6 cm..........
.................................61˙7 cm...............................

Figure 10

FACE D OF ROD: SPEAKING LENGTHS.

The lengths of this scale are given below in centimetres. The distance from the upper bridge at which each string is struck — that is, the strike-proportion—is also given. The strike proportion is shown by the smaller figures.

Speaking Lengths and Strike Proportions of Strings for a Boudoir Grand Piano.

Note No.	C	B	A#	A	G#	G	F#	F	E	D#	D	C#
88	5·2 ·4	5·6 ·4	5·9 ·5	6·2 ·5	6·5 ·5	6·8 5·	7·2 ·5	7·6 ·6	8·0 ·6	8·4 ·6	8·9 ·7	9·4 ·7
76	9·9 ·7	10·4 ·8	11·0 ·9	11·6 ·9	12·3 1·0	13·0 1·0	13·7 1·1	14·4 1·2	15·3 1·3	16·1 1·3	16·9 1·4	17·9 1·5
64	18·9 1·7	19·9 1·8	20·9 1·9	22·0 2·1	23·2 2·2	24·4 2·4	25·7 2·6	27·1 2·8	28·6 3·0	30·1 3·2	31·7 3·5	33·6 3·8
52	35·3 4·0	37·3 4·3	39·4 4·6	41·7 4·9	44·0 5·2	46·4 5·5	49·0 6·0	51·6 6·3	54·5 6·7	57·3 7·1	60·4 7·5	63·4 7·9
40	66·8 8·4	70·3 8·8	73·9 9·3	77·6 9·8	80·9 10·2	84·4 10·6	87·9 11·0	91·5 11·5	94·8 11·9	98·1 12·2	100·7 12·6	102·6 12·9
28	103·8 13·1	104·9 13·2	105·7 13·5	**96·1*** 12·0	98·0 12·3	99·7 12·5	101·4 12·6	103·1 12·9	104·7 13·1	106·1 13·2	107·5 13·4	109·0 13·6
16	110·3 13·9	111·5 14·0	112·6 14·1	113·6 14·2	114·5 14·3	115·4 14·4	116·1 14·5	116·8 14·7	117·4 14·7	117·9 14·7	118·3 14·8	118·7 14·9
4	119·0 14·9	119·2 15·0	119·4 15·1	119·5 15·1								

* Bass section from A^1 to A^{25}.

At C^{88} the strike proportion is shown as one-thirteenth of the total string length. At C^{64} it is one-eleventh. At C^{52}, one-ninth. At C^{40} it is about one-eighth; and in the bass section it is also one-eighth.

Figure 9 shows the scale drawing for the horizontal instrument under examination. The illustration also shows the markings on the faces of the scale stick. The markings on face D for the bass string lengths are carried round to the unused part of face C, this being done to avoid confusion with the longer treble string markings.

In preparing the actual drawing (see Fig. 9), a line is drawn for each note from the point marked on the bottom scales to, and to a certain unfixed distance beyond, the strike point, each line passing through the centre of the note which it represents on the strike scale. The strike-proportion for each note is then set out beneath the strike-line (E). These markings provide the points through which a line is drawn: this line representing the upper limit of the speaking lengths, and thus the top-bridge position, and the position for the agraffes.

The next step is to mark off the speaking length of each string from face D of the scale rod. This completed, it is possible to indicate the soundboard bridge scale. An important point is that, when marking the width of trichord and bichord notes on the soundboard bridges, the width must be marked parallel to the small segment of the top-bridge curve. It is only by having the length of each string of a note exactly similar that an equality of tension can be obtained. A tiny error can result in the strings of one note varying in tension as much as 10 lb.

The total width of the notes on the soundboard bridges varies throughout the compass. Each string on a piano would, were it not for the two rows of soundboard bridge-pins, run without deflection from wrest-pin coil or from the top bearing to the hitch pin. It is of assistance to remember that each string is continually endeavouring to overcome the resistance of the bridge-pins. And this tendency exerts a twisting strain on the soundboard bridges. Experiments have proved that the strain on the bridges due to the angle made by the strings between the rows of pins amounts to about 60 lb. in each direction per trichord *note*. Adhesion of the strings to the soundboard bridges is created partly by "down-bearing," but also by the side-draft which follows when a string is passed round a bridge pin. The draft depends on three things: the semi-diameter of the wire, the semi-diameter of the pin, and the small overhang of the pin.   The string is brought back to its original direction by the lower row of bridge pins.   The wires cut slightly into the bridge-surface : about one-eighth of the diameter of the wire is embedded in the wood.   For evidence of this, note the deep impression made by the heavier steels at the foot of the long bridge of any piano.

A complete drawing of the construction of a piano, and one from which working templates could be made, would show, in addition to the actual scale, the iron frame, the details of the soundboard. and also the piano back.   These four units should be picked out in different coloured ink.   Separate drawings showing the placement of the action and keys, and the design of the case-work would also be necessary.

CHAPTER VII

The Iron Frame

INTRODUCTION.

THE thin, light and wiry tone of dulcimers, clavichords, virginals and spinets was due, in part, to the very small "mass" of wire which was set in vibration. The strings of the earlier clavier instruments were of *iron* in the tenor and treble sections, and brass and copper in the bass part. This iron wire was so soft that it was easily wrapped around the wrest pins by the fingers of the stringer; the wrest pins were not drilled, the wire being crossed over the coils. The low tenacity of the wire prevented it from being stretched at a tension which would yield a full, round tone. The frames of the early grand and square pianos were constructed entirely of wood, the total stress due to the tension of the strings being very small.

The continual improvement in the elasticity and tenacity of *steel* wire[12] has made possible the modern piano. To provide a wooden structure capable of bearing the increased stress of instruments strung with steel wire was, for the piano makers of that time, an almost insuperable problem. But when iron was added to wood in piano structure, a new era was inaugurated in piano making.

[12] Steel wire was made in Wales as early as 1735, but the iron wire of the German wire-smiths, made by the *drawing* process, was used for musical instruments until Brockedon (in 1819) introduced the idea of drawing wire through holes in diamonds and rubies. The iron wire might have withstood a string tension of 60 lb. To-day, the average string tension is about 170 lb., giving a total stress on the structure of possibly 17 tons against 3 or 4 tons for the old square piano, Steinway, in their 1924 catalogue, state that their grands have a total string tension of 60,000 pounds,—say 27 tons. What is interesting about the early instruments is that the stability of the tuning was very poor. Half-way through a performance, while the artists relaxed, the services of a tuner were required to bring the instrument into tune again.

HISTORICAL.

While the first use of iron in the structure of pianos is the result not so much of the idea of a single individual as the gradual growth from the suggestions of many workers, there are two names which must always be associated with the beginnings of the iron frame in the modern piano.

First, John Isaac Hawkins, an Englishman residing in America, who in 1800 patented a full iron frame. Then Alpheus Babcock, an American, who in 1825 took out a patent for a metal frame with a hitch-pin plate made in one casting. Other workers in the same direction were Joseph Smith, William Allen (a tuner in the employment of Stodart), Pierre Erard, Henry Fowler Broadwood, and Jonas Chickering of Boston: but it is generally acceded that the battle for the iron frame was not won until Steinway & Sons in 1855 demonstrated at New York that over-strung scaling with a solid iron frame could yield the desired volume and quality of tone. American manufacturers claim with just pride that, when exhibiting in London, in 1862, their pianos with the full iron frame were recognised as marking a definite development in piano manufacture.

Siegfried Hansing,[13] in the 1904 edition of his work, "The Pianoforte and its Acoustic Properties," wrote :—

"Although piano construction in foreign lands is arranged according to the American system, especially among the Germans (who have not hesitated to send their sons to America to study piano making), it is safe to assert that American cast iron frames are superior to all others in quality and artistic construction. The arched forms of the plates between the iron bars, which stand out from the rims of the frames much like the form of a violin, render a sufficient resisting power against the drawing of the strings possible with a casting only 7 mm. thick......

" Some piano builders have lately been thinking much of aluminium frames for pianos. Aluminium is said to be three times lighter than iron, but it is very doubtful whether the properties of aluminium are superior to those of cast iron or not as regards its use for the purpose of metal frames in pianos.

" Let us faithfully and carefully guard the cast iron frame, for it is not likely that another metal will be found which during the process of casting will shrink so little as does cast iron. With 95 cm., cast iron shrinks only

[13] Hansing was a German with considerable knowledge of American methods of piano making. His book was written in the German language and has been translated in part by various Englishmen ; but Hansing was not satisfied, and later the book was translated into English by his daughter (Emmy Hansing-Perzina). This is the edition best known in England. It must be said that the full meaning of the author is often obscured by a want of lucidity in the translation.

about 1 cm., so that the shrinking quotient is about 1·0104. What other
metal could replace cast iron with so small a shrinking quotient? Yet even
this slight shrinking of cast iron so changes the form and proportions of the
iron frame that the scale maker who in making the wooden model has not
calculated with the shrinking quotient of cast iron has to alter the stringing scale according to the form and proportions of the iron frame. Hereby
the carefully calculated and worked plan of the stringing scale is lost, and
the scale maker is compelled to adopt dimensions in the scale which he
would otherwise have refused to accept.

"The first cast iron frame which comes from the mould made after the
wooden model is kept in the iron foundry to be used as a model for casting
other frames to be used in pianos. Therefore, in making the wooden
model a double shrinking quotient must be employed in the calculation.
If iron, in shrinking once, diminishes from 97 cm. to 96 cm., it will dim-
inish from 97 cm. down to 95 cm. in shrinking twice; therefore the double
shrinking quotient is 97 : 95 = 1·02."

Hansing treated everything with an impartial and unbiased
keenness of perception. He was, of course, a thoroughly practical
piano maker and a master of his art.

THE MODERN FRAME.

Time was when people imagined that the presence of iron in a
piano caused a metallic tone, and that the best tone came from
the wooden framed pianos. To-day it is not all who realise that
iron is used only as a stress-resisting structure, the full tone now
general being due to the high tension of the wires. Yet, to a very
slight extent, the pressure of the wire on the fixed upper lip-
bridge of the iron frame transmits the vibrations of the strings to
the frame itself: thence it passes to the wooden frame-work of
the piano and to the floor of the room. A sharp difference between
the volume and resonance of treble notes is due, at times, to the
frame being more responsive to certain pitches.

The art of piano making is peculiarly dependent upon ancil-
lary industries. The casting of iron frames for pianos is perhaps
the most important auxiliary industry, because the frame-design
strikes at the very basis of the piano,—that is, at·the scale-design.
There are many examples in modern instruments of scales being
adapted to fit existing frames. The frame and the scale of a
piano are not separate entities. Once the frame is designed from
a scale drawing, it can be suitably embellished, and the whole
given a pleasing and artistic appearance, cast iron lending itself
to ornamentation. This artistic form and finish to the frame can
be varied in different castings, though both may retain the same
scaling.

A piano-scale (which is the placement of the bearings, the

wrest pins, the bridges, and the string-lengths) finds its way into the finished piano in the form of the iron frame. The dimensions of the cast frame[14] determine the position of practically all the other elements of the piano.

A complete scale-drawing would show the front elevation of the frame.

A few of the more interesting facts concerning the iron frame may be discussed here.

CONTRACTION—The allowance usually made between the contraction drawing and the actual frame is two per cent. A very high quality of iron is required for piano frames. The wooden pattern made by the piano maker is only used to enable a standard iron one to be cast. When smoothed, this is the permanent iron pattern for the foundry. Two allowances have to be made: (a) between the wooden pattern and the first iron frame; and (b) between the first iron pattern and the finished product. But two per cent. suffices. In making a contraction drawing, face dimensions only need to be expanded. Thicknesses should be left "bare," because, when the pattern is extracted from the sand mould, it has to be "rapped" (i.e., shaken) to enable it to be withdrawn without damage to the mould. This "rapping" causes a thickening. *Draw*: all parts of the frame have to be given a "draw" or tapering to prevent damage to the sand mould. About 1 in 96 is said to be the minimum, though obviously the more that can be given the cleaner will be the casting. A distinct "draw" can be given to a piano frame. This "draw" is not all in one direction; the parts which are moulded in the iron-founder's upper box draw in the reverse direction, and these should have a greater "draw" than the remainder; the reason being that it is more difficult to remove the sand-packed upper frame with safety. If a pronounced "draw" or taper is given to the wrest-plank rebate, this ridge should be planed before the frame leaves the foundry.

PATTERN MAKING.—The making of a frame pattern calls for considerable skill, both in design and craftsmanship. The finished pattern must be most carefully cornered and varnished.

WEIGHT OF CASTING.— A convenient way of estimating the weight of a casting is to divide the specific gravity of cast-iron (7·4) by the specific gravity of the wood. For example, a frame might come out seventeen or eighteen times heavier than a pattern made with whitewood.

---

[14] In Canada and the United States, the cast-iron frame is known as the _piano plate_, in France *cadre en fer*, and in Germany *platte*.

INTERNAL STRESS. — The danger of internal stress in a piano frame is overcome by the foundry turning out a frame with a very large safety factor: possibly as high as two or three hundred per cent. But it is often thought that the internal stress has an effect upon the ultimate tone of the instrument. A rod will vibrate and yield the 29th partial tone, which can be quite audible; and bodies under torsion vibrate with a large number of enharmonic partial tones. Metal under stress loses certain qualities: it becomes "fatigued." It is possible that a change occurs in the molecular structure of the metal. Frames which have a large internal stress will frequently snap at the bars during transport. Makers of piano frames are endeavouring always by a better distribution of the metal, by a better compromise of tension and compression members, and by better foundry practice to eliminate internal stress. The piano frame is the "backbone" of the instrument, and the casting of this skeleton of bars, which has an immense cooling surface and which gains its strength from a scientific distribution of the metal rather than from bulk, is considered an achievement in foundry practice.

TEMPERATURE MOVEMENT. — The movements of a piano frame due to changes of temperature are fortunately coincident with those of the cast-steel piano wire. There is thus a compensating action. If, due to very hot weather, the frame expands, and there is an increase in tension and pitch, the steel wire also expands with a compensating drop in tension and therefore in pitch. A fall in temperature contracts the wire and increases the pitch, but the bars of the frame also contract practically to the same degree: and thus the tension and pitch is lowered. It is because of these facts that a high-grade modern piano will always stand up to pitch: and, while it will always require fine-tuning, there is seldom a vibration of pitch (sharp or flat) beyond three or four vibrations in the frequency per second.

STRIKE LINE.—An excessive width of the notes at the strike, and thus of the frame, entails a large key splay to enable the back scale of the keys to coincide with the action scale. Excessive key splay means undue wear and a poorer touch. The front key scale cannot be varied.

BLOW LINE.—As a regular blow is preferable and enables the action to be set up square, it is necessary to recede the bass plate of the wrest plank, this partly to compensate for the thickness of the lower covered strings. The hammers which strike the steels are usually about $\frac{1}{4}$ in. to $\frac{5}{16}$ in. shorter than those of the bass section, this maintaining a standard blow throughout the range.

BARS. — There is no reason why the number of " strike-line breaks" in the upright frame should be limited to two. In high-grade pianos, it is general to find two bars in the treble section. Bass-bar: adequate provision has to be made for the wide movement of the lowest note ; the bass-bar must never be made nearer than $\frac{3}{4}$in. to the centre of the string diameter of A^1. The head-bar must always allow room for the collar of the tuner's hammer to turn.

In upright pianos, the bars of the iron frame should be so dimensioned and positioned as to place as much as possible of the resistance in the line of the stress. The height of the soundboard bridge prevents this being done entirely. The idea has been expressed that bars in upright frames may be regarded as columns. In grands they become inverted girders.

The bars of grand frames are very deep relative to the width: this because the strength of a girder varies directly as the *square* of the depth. Cast iron is exceedingly strong against a direct *crushing* force, but is comparatively weak against a tensile strain. An average of the published figures of the strength of cast iron is : resistance to compressive strain, 50 tons per square inch ; resistance to tensional strain, 7 to 8 tons per square inch.[15]

It is probably true that scrap iron makes the better material for iron frames, as repeated meltings increase the tensile strength. The ideal metal is that which is of high tensile strength, and is tough, yet not too tough, otherwise the drilling operations are impeded. If the metal is very tough, it will not be fluid enough to fill the delicate ornaments sometimes found on grand frames. Such ornaments are better cast separately from more fluid iron, and subsequently screwed into position.

The bars of the upright frame are generally in tension on the back edge. It is considered good foundry practice to add flanges to this edge : therefore most bars of uprights are really **T** section columns. The under face of grand frame bars are in compression, and no addition of strength is necessary. The position of the bars of the grand frame prevents any cutting away of the bridges, which, however, cannot be avoided in the upright piano, as the bars must stand in the space between the strings and the action, their depth being limited accordingly.

[15] Compare this with steel piano wire, which will stand up to 150 tons per square inch.

BEARINGS.— The stud was first introduced to prevent the blows of the hammers in grand pianos from driving the strings up and away from their bearings on the old-time wood wrest-plank bridge. The bearing of the strings in the studs was against the upper side of the holes. For the extreme treble register of grands, the cast-in bearing-bar is now general, it being difficult to find sufficient room for studs. The grand stud is useless for the upright piano, for the precise reason which makes it so desirable in the horizontal instrument,— namely, the hammer blows tend to unseat the bearing of the string. The double-bearing upright stud, when finally screwed into the frame, makes an ideal, if expensive, upper bearing. A stud-bearing automatically spaces the strings; it readily permits of a deflection of the line of the string between upper bridge and wrest-pins (the lowest bass notes can seldom be permitted to continue in the line of speaking-length, for this makes the piano excessive in width). Further, a stud-bearing allows the wrest-pin scale to be closer to the bridge than if a pressure-bar is employed. The stud provides a means of exactly fixing the "down-bearing."

Fig. 11 illustrates the single bearing grand stud and the double bearing stud of the upright piano.

Figure 11

The four studs illustrated in Fig. 12 are interesting. The first, reading from left to right, is the trichord grand stud with an inset steel bearing. This small piece of inset metal is round and of about 2 mm. diameter, thus giving a good bearing of 1 mm.: which bearing can be worked to an exact radius in the manufacture of the stud. This combination of a brass stud with a harder metal bearing surface is not new; in fact, this type of stud was imported into England from France some fifty years ago. The ordinary grand stud, and also the double bearing *upright* stud, were used much earlier still, notably by Collard and Kirkman. The second stud in Fig. 12 is the double bearing grand stud. This stud is still to be found in the extreme treble of the high-grade grands of one or two renowned makers. The stud is given a distinct rake, which carries its centre farther from the wrest-plank edge, and also gives a better clearance for the treble hammers. This stud, and in fact all the four, can be fitted with the steel bearing bar. The third stud illustrated is one which is not often seen. It is used by some German manufacturers. Its outstanding advantage is that the width of a note at the bearing (and also at the strike) can be varied, thereby overcoming a small disadvantage of the ordinary stud. Further, one type serves for the single string, the

Figure 12

bichord and the trichord. A second bearing would be necessary with this stud. The last illustration shows a double bearing upright stud. Some makers have studs of their own design, to meet their own types of bearings. Blüthner uses a very beautifully made stud for the aliquot scaling. This stud has a fourth bearing slightly higher than those of the struck strings. The bearing of the unstruck string at the belly bridge is made by a very delicate stud, which is screwed into the wood of the bridge.

The iron frame has to be drilled and tapped very accurately for the stud positions. Studs, being of brass, are softer than the iron bridge, and the bearing part of the stud can be easily worked to an exact radius,—generally about $\frac{1}{16}$ in. There is no danger of rusting at the point of contact, whereas with the iron bridge rust will sometimes develop at the point of bearing with the strings, and this makes delicacy of movement, which is the essential of fine tuning, quite impossible. Another feature in favour of the stud is that it can be so set as to coincide with the squaring off of the lower end of the speaking length of each note: that is, with the notching of the belly bridge. The speaking length and the strike proportion of the three strings of one note are thus exactly identical. The ideal bearing is one which permits of the purest and the longest continuance of tone due to the vibrations not passing the limit of the active length. The one disadvantage of the stud is that the bearing cannot be lubricated. Stringers can reduce friction by using wax at all the upper bearings. A piano fitted with studs requires greater care and skill in the stringing operations.

It must be mentioned that the stud is, of course, an expensive adjunct to the frame.

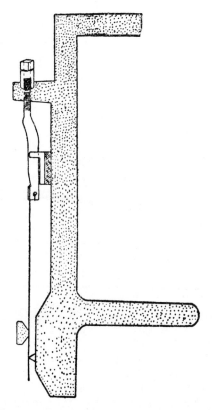

Figure 13

Fig. 13 illustrates a form of upper bearing patented many years ago by an eminent American firm of piano makers (Mason & Hamlin). The wood wrest-plank is entirely eliminated, the string being held by a travelling plunger. The head of the plunger carries a nut; this nut is turned by a tuning hammer having a special collar, the tension and pitch of the speaking length is varied as the tuner's ear decides.

Fig. 14 shows an arrangement of levels for the top bearing of a grand.

Additional bearings between *studs* and the wrest pins are sometimes used, especially if the angle which the string would make between the stud-bearing and the wrest-pin coil is insufficient to check the vibrations. Strings in passing the upper bridge should give an angle of not less than 15 degrees. In Fig. 14 the additional bearing is of half-round brass.

Additional bearings between a pressure bar and the wrest pins are quite unnecessary. Such bearings create additional friction, render fine and permanent tuning — i.e., "firm" tuning — difficult; and, if the adhesion is considerable, they cause strings to snap. A cushion or felt bearing, or a piece of heavy listing entwined between the strings, will effectively silence sympathetic vibrations in the top dead-string lengths.

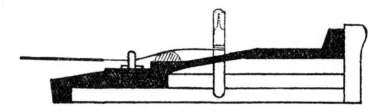

Figure 14

In a renowned make of piano, the dead-lengths of string are given a definite open length, so that, it is claimed, they may be free to vibrate with the active length. While it is impossible to control the tension and pitch of these small lengths of wire, it is not improbable that the vibrations of the speaking length compel a certain movement in the back string. If, as in grands, the extra vibrating length is below the long bridge, a sympathy of movement is bound to be transmitted from the bridge itself. If the open length is at the top bearing, the degree of movement of the additional wire would depend on the angle made by the string in passing the stud or the cast-in bearing bar.

Figure 1, shown on page 36 of this book, illustrates clearly the two forms of top bearings now generally used in upright pianos.

STRING ANGLES.—A decision must always be made, and the frame design modified accordingly, covering the angle which the strings are to make with the vertical. It is customary so to secure the frames of upright pianos to the back that the spun strings are vertical and the steels slightly inclined. This inclination tends to prevent the bending of the hammer shanks and also prevents the hammer face "wandering" up the string. A stroking movement of the hammer is very undesirable. The degree to which the bass strings are elevated from the steels governs the construction of the wood-back. Bracings are sometimes reduced in thickness at the bottom to allow the frame to give a vertical position for the covered strings. The back-liners of the piano should, of course, be in line with the vertical. The angle made between the two sets of strings can be about 1in. in 4ft.

It is usually assumed that the steels in grand pianos are — downbearing angles being ignored—quite horizontal.

ELEVATION OF BASS SECTION.—The bass section of a frame has to be elevated so that at the strike there is $\frac{5}{16}$in. distance between the strings. The excursions of the very flexible strings at either side of the bass-break must be considered. If these are both struck heavily at the same time, there is a very wide movement. The wrest-plank and hitch-plate levels of the frame must conform to give from $\frac{3}{8}$in. to $\frac{3}{4}$in. distance at the point where contact of the strings is likely.

CROSSING ANGLES OF STRINGS.—The angles at which the strings cross affect not only the length of the strings, but also the position of the bridges, and thus the position of the sound-board bars. Too great an angle restricts the working space for the dampers of the break notes. An increase in the width of the break at the strike level is practicable but undesirable. An even hammer-line is to be preferred, but it is sometimes advisable to lift the strike position of four or five break notes. In such cases the upper bridge-curve must be modified to give the required strike proportion. If the "strike" of break notes is lifted to an excessive degree—say, more than half-an-inch—the increase in the length of the hammer shanks would affect the touch, the speed of the hammer being altered.

METAL WREST PLANK FACES.—The tendency to carry the bars of the frame up to the head bar and to the close in the plank face has everything to recommend it. The forward pull of the strings is borne by the bars instead of by the wooden back, and the function of the back is reduced to providing a seating for the soundboard and the wrest plank, and a means of making a secure union with the general case-work of the piano. The wood back of an upright piano should not, if the frame is suitably designed, contribute anything to the resistance of tensional strain. (The bracings of a grand, of course, serve only to support and to give rigidity to the rim.) It is inadvisable to allow wrest pins to fit the holes in metal plates. The ideal fitment is for the wrest pin holes in the frame to be deeply countersunk *from the back*, and for hard-wood plugs (i.e., bushings) to be used. The plug supports the pin: transfers the strain to the frame: it also prevents a torsional movement in the pin itself, which

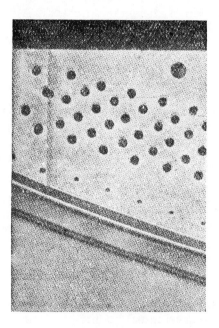

Figure 15

movement, it may be mentioned, is very embarrassing to the tuner, making it necessary for every pin to be given a "set" backwards to remove the strain. Wrest pins should be supported as close as possible to the point where the string leaves the pin. Any distance greater than $\frac{1}{8}$ in. may be regarded as excessive and causing a very great direct bending strain on the pin. In open-faced frames there is sometimes a considerable length of pin between the plank and the string as it leaves the pin. This makes the crushing strain on the underside of a hole enormous: it can be as high as 300 lb. The fibres of the wood are crushed, the holes elongated, and the dragging of the pins prevents the piano standing up to pitch.

Fig. 15 shows a wooden wrest-plank face with the holes enlarged by the strain.

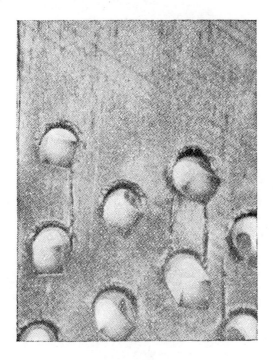

Figure 16

Fig. 16 shows how the veneer face of a plank will split and the pins drag down by a bad arrangement of the upper-bearing levels.

For use in the tropics, many forms of all-iron wrest planks have been designed. Fig. 17 shows one design, in which, instead of introducing the pins from the front. driving them in like a nail, they are put in from the back. A conical shoulder is on the end of each pin, and this shoulder fits an accurately turned conical face in the iron wrest-plank. An adjustable tension screw presses the shoulder of the pin against the conical face. The pins are lubricated with a graphite mixture and turn easily.

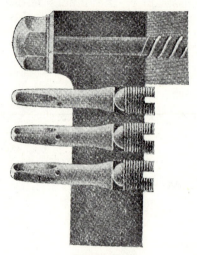

Figure 17

Fig. 18 illustrates a section of the frame and shows the immense strength of this form of construction.

Figure 18

For normal conditions, the closed-face frame with wood plugs leaves little to be desired. Fig. 19 illustrates this type of fitment for the wrest pins.

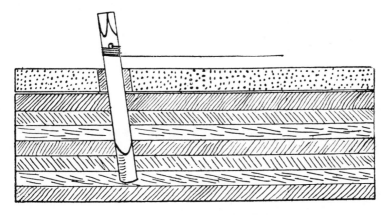

Figure 19

Metal plank plates should be drilled out about 11 mm. diameter. Plugs can then be fitted which, if the holes are countersunk from the back, permits of a drill being used to bore out both the plug and the plank in one operation.

WREST PIN ANGLES.—It is necessary that wrest pins should have a slight upward rake. If driven rectangular to the plank face, considerable embarrassment is found in tuning: this more especially if the open-faced plank is used, because, as previously stated, the holes become elongated and there is a downward slant to the pin. If a tuner employs a tee hammer, it is very difficult to prevent the hammer continually slipping off the pin. Should the upward slope of the wrest pin be excessive, there is the difficulty of keeping the three or four coils of the wire in contact with each other. A large upward slant to the pins prohibits the use of the longer crank tuning hammer, its end coming in contact with the back half-top. Five degrees is a happy compromise between these difficulties. A hammer shank inserted in the bored hole and tried against a fixed bevel of five degrees is a quick way of testing the slope. Not only should the wrest-pin holes be bored to give an upward angle to the wrest pin, but they should be bored so that the pin slopes also in the opposite direction to the pull of the strings.

HITCH-PIN POSITION.—In practice, it is found that a variation in the length of back-string has no effect upon the tone. Thus the curve of the hitch-pin plate is usually equal to the sweep of the soundboard bridge. For English (Broadwood) eyes, the hitch pin must be on the string line: but for German eyes, a set-off of $\frac{1}{16}$in. to the bass side is necessary, the eye not being central to the string.

TYPES OF FRAMES.

Fig. 20 illustrates a type of grand frame with, in all, three breaks in the strike scale. It is a type which is in general use. There is a closed wrest-plank face. The weight of a frame of this nature is about 250 lb.

Figure 20

Fig. 21 shows an early type of upright frame for a vertically strung piano. The **T** section of the bars is shown distinctly, as is also the reduction of the flange at the back edge of the treble bar, where the bar crosses the soundboard bridge.

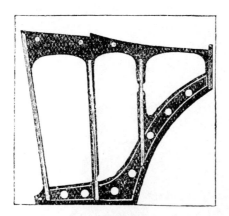

Figure 21

Fig. 22 shows an early type of upright overstrung frame. It will be noticed that the treble bar is continued upwards a little, and, in the finished piano, a screw entered the wrest plank at the head of this bar.

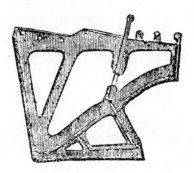

Figure 22

These two illustrations (Fig. 21 and Fig. 22) are interesting because they are reproduced from copies of *Musical Opinion* dated 1879 and 1882 respectively. Both the frames were made by Messrs. Whitfield of Birmingham.

BARLESS FRAME.—No notes on piano frames would be complete without reference to the Broadwood barless frame, which was patented in 1888 by Henry John Tschudi Broadwood. In this frame the plate is of mild or cast steel turned up round the sides to form a continuous flange. This construction meets the modern

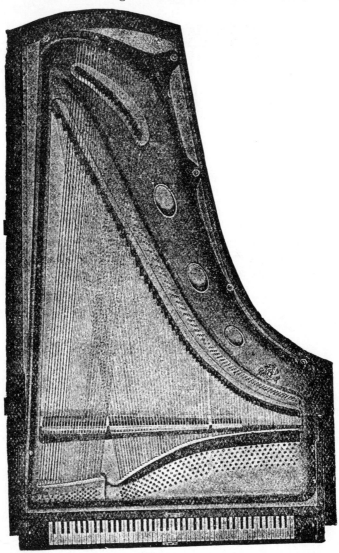

Figure 23

increase in tension without the aid of bars, and is undoubtedly
a realised ideal. Through the courtesy of Messrs. Broadwood
& Sons, we are able to reproduce an illustration of their barless
grand (Fig. 23). The outstanding advantage of the barless frame
is that it permits of an even scale.

Fig. 24 shows the Broadwood barless upright frame. A frame
constructed of cast steel upon these lines is of great comparative
lightness and stiffness, and the absence of the bars gives a greater
facility for the arrangement of the action and keys. The tone of
the piano, as a result, possesses a freedom and purity not possible where the depth of the soundboard bridge is reduced to
allow room for the frame bars.

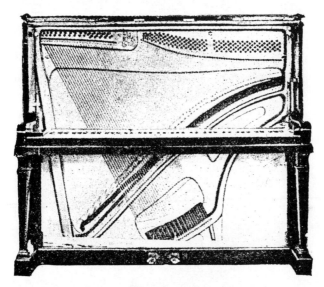

Figure 24

Fig. 25 shows a closed-in wrest plank type of frame made by
an American foundry (the Wickham Piano Plate Company of
Springfield, Ohio). The piano number is stamped on the wood
wrest plank, and a small grove is left in the casting of the plank
plate, so that the number is visible when the frame is screwed
down.

Fig. 26 is interesting : it shows the "double overstrung" frame
which to-day finds little favour. English makers never took to
the double overstrung scale, and on the Continent piano?makers
have discarded the idea.

Figure 25

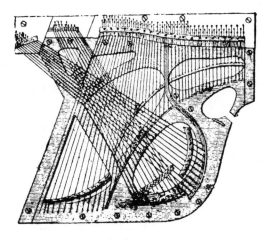

Figure 26

Fig. 27 illustrates a modern upright frame made by Messrs. Whitfield of Birmingham. This type is designed for a pressure-bar bearing; the plank faces are open, the wrest pins entering directly into the wood of the wrest plank.

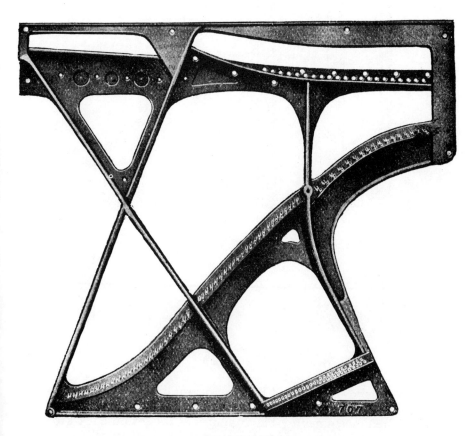

Figure 27

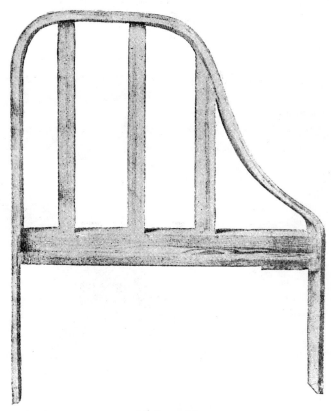

Figure 28

Fig. 28 shows the wood back of a grand. The reader should now glance at Fig. 29, which shows the grand frame embodied in the finished instrument. The bracings of the grand back are not subject to any strains due to the tension of the strings.

Mention may be made here of the fact that the use of the continuous bent rim for grand pianos has revolutionised the whole system of building grands, and has been a large factor in making possible the manufacture of the cheaper grand piano. The continuous rim enables the grand to be treated in exactly the same way as the upright, it being bellied and marked-off prior to the attachment of the case.

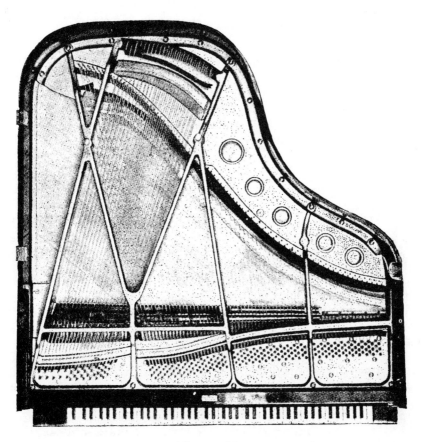

Figure 29

CHAPTER VIII

The Action

INTRODUCTION.

THE train of mechanism which transmits to the strings the impetus given by the player's touch is the action. The precursor of the piano, the dulcimer, was played by blows of hammers held in the hands of the performer.

It was Cristofori, a Paduan harpsichord maker, who first constructed the machinery through which the impulse of the finger could be transmitted to the string, and so produce either a soft or a loud tone. Thus it is true that the action of Cristofori really marks the invention of the pianoforte *quâ* piano-e-forte.

The piano keyboard and the mechanical apparatus called the action are the means of agitating the steel strings which constitute the prime sound-producing element of the instrument. The front end of a piano key is capable of depression up to three-eighths of an inch. This figure is technically known as touch. Some Continental makers give a shallower touch,—at times, only six millimetres. If a piano has a total touch of ten millimetres, nine would constitute the working depth, which is just sufficient to carry the hammer to the string. The small additional depth, together with the degree to which the baize pad beneath the front of the key is compressed, allows for escapement and the locking of the check head with the balance hammer. This after-touch is apparent to the player because a tiny increase of pressure is necessary to complete the full depression of the key. The rear end of the key which meets the action travels up about a quarter of an inch.

The means of stopping the sound—that is, of damping—is included in the action.

The piano action must also be regarded as the vehicle by which the pedals possess the ability to sustain and modify

72

the quality of the tone. A single key governs its corresponding action unit, but the pedal governs the damping of the whole instrument.

NOMENCLATURE.

Digression may be made for a moment to mention the names of action parts. Such words as butt, rocker, centre, bell-crank lever, spoon, carriage, bridle, tape, slap-rail, escapement, flange (or flinge), beam, rider, &c., call for no explanation. Other words, like prologue (or prolonge), abstract, hopper, wippen and jack are interesting.

The complete action is called by the French *mécanique*, by the Germans *mechanik*, and in the home of its birth (Italy) it is known as *mecanica*.

Hopper came from the fact that the wood "hopped" out from under the notch and allowed the hammer to fall clear away from the string. The hopper of the jack in Cristofori's action was called by the inventor, *linguetta mobile*.

Jack is simply English for lever and is at least as old as Shakespeare, who says,

> Do I envy those jacks that nimble leap
> To kiss the tender inward of thy hand.

The couplet is from Sonnet CXXVIII. It might perhaps be said that Shakespeare has mixed his technicalities. The reference, however, is of course to the jack as a key-lever of the Elizabethan virginals. This will be seen from a reading of the complete sonnet.

> How oft, when thou, my music, music play'st,
> Upon that blessed wood whose motion sounds
> With thy sweet fingers, when thou gently sway'st
> The wiry concord that mine ear confounds,
> Do I envy those jacks that nimble leap
> To kiss the tender inward of thy hand,
> Whilst my poor lips, which should that harvest reap,
> At the wood's boldness by thee blushing stand !
> To be so tickl'd, they would change their state
> And situation with those dancing chips,
> O'er whom thy fingers walk with gentle gait,
> Making dead wood more bless'd than living lips,
>> Since saucy jacks so happy are in this,
>> Give them thy fingers, me thy lips to kiss.

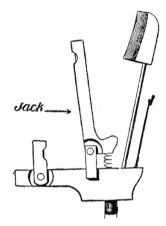

Figure 30

The jack of the modern upright action is shown clearly in Fig. 30.

Wippen may have come from the verb "to wipe" = to take a swinging stroke.   The French use the term *taquet-propulseur* (forcing pin) for wippen. The jack-head, which attacks the notch, is still called the hopper or sometimes the fly.

To-day, by *wippen* is understood the whole of the under-part of the action section.   Both the grand and the upright action consist of two sharply distinct units.   The lower wippen section is entirely free from the upper section, which moves forward and meets the strings.

Fig. 31 shows a grand wippen.

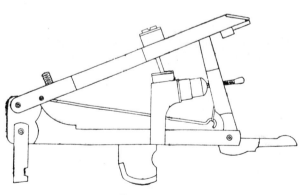

Figure 31

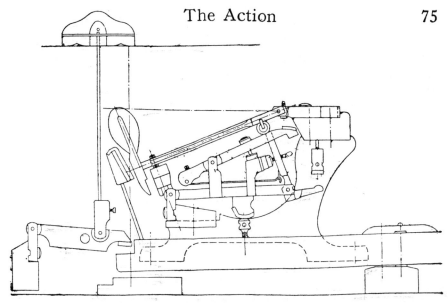

Figure 32

Fig. 32 shows a complete grand section. (The unit shown is from the Schwander B action.)

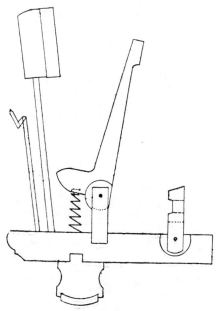

Figure 33

Fig. 33 illustrates the upright wippen, and the complete

upright unit is shown in Fig. 34. In this illustration, the two sections of a unit are shown assembled upon the action beam. The permanently rigid parts of the action should be noted: they are the beam (B), the set-off rail and button (R), and the butt and wippen flanges (F).

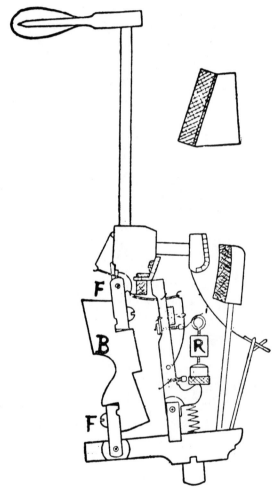

Fig. 34

(Note that the jack has completed its attack upon the notch

While the lower section or wippen of the grand is *completely* independent from its hammer section (see Figs. 36 and 37, page 80), the two sections of the upright action are connected by a tape, which is loosely regulated, and is — in actions fitted with the half-blow attachment — quite otiose. The tape is useful, however, when the action is removed from the piano case, as it prevents the jack-head dropping behind the notch, and in damp situations it undoubtedly assists the return of the hammer. The introduction of this tie (sometimes called a bridle) goes back to the "double" or "piccolo" action of Robert Wornum (1826); but the expression "tape-action" is, of course, still in common use.

.   .   .   .

The essentials of a good action, we prefer to think, may be presented thus :—

> (*a*) There must be absolute control over the blow, enabling its intensity and so the volume of tone to be varied with facility and certainty.

> (*b*) There must be immediate withdrawal of the hammer from the string, otherwise the hammer becomes a damper. (The hammer should leave the string as a golf ball would come up when bounced on a hard surface.)

> (*c*) This withdrawal must be irrespective of whether the player continues the depression of the key or otherwise.

> (*d*) Once the blow is struck, there must be no bouncing backwards or forwards of the hammer. The hammer must not only leave the string, but must be checked. Yet—

> (*e*) —there must be the facility for immediate and continuing repetition of the note, should the player so desire.

> (*f*) This repetition must be fully possible whether the key has returned to its normal level or not.

> (*g*) The right-hand pedal must raise and lower each and every damper instantaneously and without noise.

Truly a formidable list. Yet the grand action fulfils these duties very nearly to perfection.

The Grand Action.

Fig. 35 shows a unit of the modern "double-escapement" grand action. It will be apparent that damping in the grand is under the immediate control of the key itself. Observe the points 1, 16, 20 and 15 in the drawing. (The damper in the upright action has to be controlled *via* the wippen, the damper spoon, and a lever centred upon the action beam.) A reference to points 7, 11 and 1 (Fig. 35) will show that "checking" in the grand is also under the immediate control of the key.

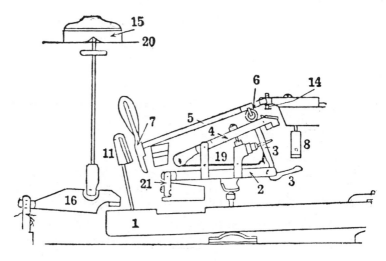

Figure 35

There is an impression prevalent among some players that the two pedals of the grand piano cannot be employed at the same moment. A glance at points 16 and 1 (Fig. 35) will prove that, whether the keyboard has moved laterally, due to the depression of the soft pedal or not, there is no interference with the lifting by the sustaining pedal of all damper levers (16) of the action. Certain it is that composers continually demand the use of the sustaining pedal in *pianissimo* passages.

A brief explanation of Fig. 35 is that the end of key 1 (not shown) lifts wippen 2. The key also carries check-head 11, which checks the hammer after the blow; further, the key governs the movement of damper 15 through the medium of 16 and damper flange 21.

The wippen 2 moves on its flange 21, and causes the jack 3 to attack the roller 6. The player's intention and individuality is imparted to the roller and thence to the hammer. The shank 5 holds the hammer head 7.

Just before the head 7 meets the string 20, the jack "bell-crank arm" 3 meets the pad 8. Being centred on 2, the jack is thus freed from the roller 6. Escapement is said to have taken place.

The lever 4, when the unit is not in use, supports the roller 6, the spring 19 maintaining the contact. A gentle depression of the key will show that this lever 4 moves up with the general rise of the wippen. The padded extremity of the arm 4 meeting the under-face of button 14, enables the jack-head at the latest moment to impart its impulse to the roller, and so to the hammer. It is the meeting of points 3 and 8 which enables the attacking jack to break clear from that part of the action which hits the strings.

The hammer section (5, 6, 7), after meeting the strings, is "cushioned" back by meeting the repetition arm 4, and is further supported by check head 11 for a repetition of the blow.

It is all these factors which produce the ideal touch, blow, damping and repetition of the horizontal instrument.

The expression "double escapement," as applied to the grand action, is misleading and is a misnomer. There can be only one escapement for the attacking jack (observe the points 3, 6 and 8 of Fig. 35). "Compound-escapement" action would be more correct, because, although the jack can only once free itself during the blow, the lever 4 escapes from contact with the roller 6, this taking place in a properly regulated unit immediately before 3 meets 8. The spring 19 has to be capable of a nice regulation, so that the repetition arm adequately supports the hammer section, yet this arm must not hinder the transference of power between the jack and the roller. The button 14 can be finely regulated to prevent the arm 4 rising too high and blocking the hammer on the strings.

As previously stated, all modern actions consist of two sections: the wippen section driving the hammer section forward, and then "escaping" before the strings are struck. The complete independence of the two sections of the grand action unit is illustrated by Figure 36 and Figure 37.

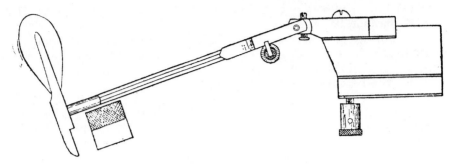

Figure 36

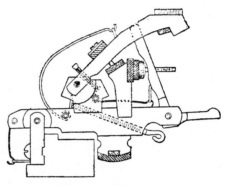

Figure 37

THE UPRIGHT ACTION.

Fig. 38 shows a unit of a modern upright action. The key movement lifts pilot P. The wippen is represented by A (flanged at T) and J. Moving up from T, the lever drives up the pivoted jack J. The jack head attacks the butt B, which carries forward the hammer to the string F. The bell-crank portion of J comes into contact with the set-off button Q, causing the jack to rotate on its centre and free itself from the butt B. The setting-off, which is another name for escapement, should take place before the hammer meets the string. The inertia of the hammer causes it to strike the string. The hammer then recoils, and, to prevent dancing, its balance hammer C is checked by E. While C is gripped by the check head E, the hammer is held and cannot bounce back: also the jack has time to drop back in readiness for a further effort.

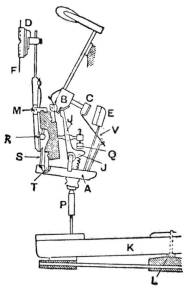

Figure 38

Now the performer has a complete command over the checking, and therefore over the return of the jack. So long as the key is kept down, the points E and C are in contact. The damper D is governed by the spoon-piece S (M is a fixed centre). The small circle (R) shown between the damper arm and the central beam-piece represents a metal rod. The right pedal of the piano moves this rod out, and so lifts all the dampers. The wippen is under control after the work of the hammer is completed; and, as the wippen controls the rise and fall of the damper, it is the upward and returning movement of the key which controls the damping of the sounds produced. The return to rest of the key lowers the wippen with its attendant damper.

The dynamics of the piano action are small circular motions governed from fixed points known as centres. These centres are really hinges made by brass pins fixed inside a bushing of very finely graded cloth.

The chief concern of the action designer is to see that all the motions of connecting sections shall be rolling motions. There must be no sliding motions, as this means noise, friction and undue wear. An instance may be given from Fig. 38. What is the ideal position for the blackleaded head of pilot P, and the felted underface of the heel of jack-lever A ?   P rotates from the fulcrum L, and A rotates from the centre T.   Therefore the contact point must be on a line joining T L.   There are further factors, however, to be considered :—

> The contact of the points P and A should be on this line throughout the whole motion of the key.

> The sharps (i.e., the raised black keys) have a different fulcrum position to that of the naturals, but a similar pilot position.

> The curvature of both the jack-lever heel and the pilot-head should be determined from the line T L.

It is axiomatic that only by compromise can the satisfactory working of the whole be accomplished.

A point to be carefully observed is that the working surfaces of action units have to be capable of exact regulation.

Actions, being made of organic material, are sensitive, and allowance has always to be made for the absorption of moisture.

The contact between the damper-spoon (S, Fig. 38) and damper-arm should be on the line which joins the two centres M and T. The design of the damper spoon and of the set-off must permit a regulation of the action which will prevent the stems of the dampers from beginning to move at the same moment as the set-off buttons (Q) come into contact with the jacks. If these two movements are coincident, there is an objectionable and sudden increase in the touch.

The considerations which apply to points P A (Fig. 38) apply also to the contact at J and Q. In other words, if the weight of the after-touch is to be almost unnoticeable, as it should be, the meeting of bell-crank lever J, with the set-off felt of Q, must be on a line, joining T and the jack-body centre. Observe here the dual movement of the jack *quâ* jack. There is an upward movement, followed by a continued upward and outward path. The shape of the jack-head (the fly) and the notch should facilitate the transference of the utmost power with the least noise and friction. The notch is made of doeskin (1 in Fig. 39), as it has to endure considerable wear. It is padded with felt (2) to prevent noise. The back of the notch (3) is of soft felt, as this merely receives the jack after the blow is given.

The butt (B, Fig. 39) has a single padded notch. Sometimes two and three pads are used.

Fig. 40 shows a different type of butt, in which the tape passes

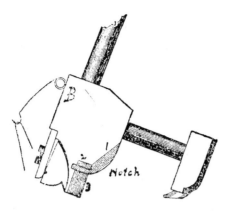

Figure 39

through a groove in an extension of the balance-hammer. If the sweep of the notch is too sharp, there is an objectionable loose-ness of touch when the half-blow (i.e., soft) pedal is used.

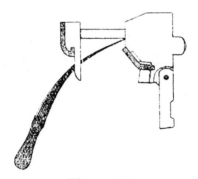

Figure 40

The *wippen* of the upright action has three additional functions to that of the grand action. Besides transmitting the energy given to the key by the player, it has to (1) control the checking, (2) govern the damping, and (3) sometimes to assist the return of the hammer and butt. These differences are important. In the grand, of course, the *key* governs both (1) and (2) while the hammer returns to rest by its own accord.

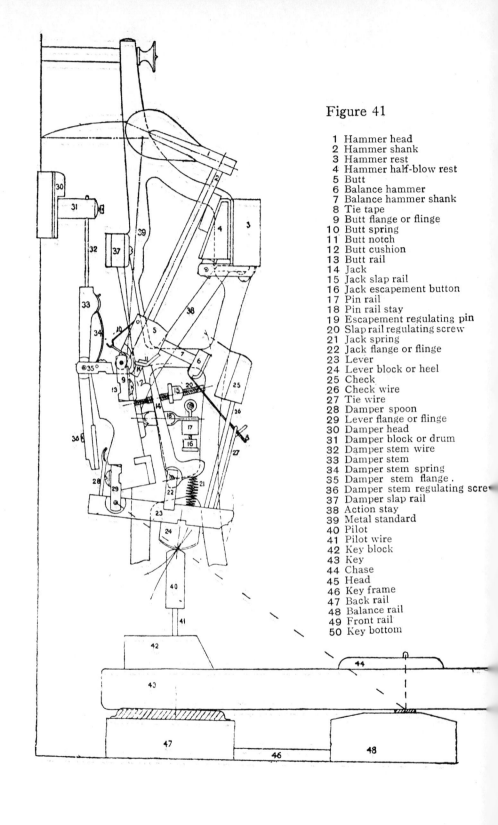

Figure 41

1 Hammer head
2 Hammer shank
3 Hammer rest
4 Hammer half-blow rest
5 Butt
6 Balance hammer
7 Balance hammer shank
8 Tie tape
9 Butt flange or flinge
10 Butt spring
11 Butt notch
12 Butt cushion
13 Butt rail
14 Jack
15 Jack slap rail
16 Jack escapement button
17 Pin rail
18 Pin rail stay
19 Escapement regulating pin
20 Slap rail regulating screw
21 Jack spring
22 Jack flange or flinge
23 Lever
24 Lever block or heel
25 Check
26 Check wire
27 Tie wire
28 Damper spoon
29 Lever flange or flinge
30 Damper head
31 Damper block or drum
32 Damper stem wire
33 Damper stem
34 Damper stem spring
35 Damper stem flange.
36 Damper stem regulating screw
37 Damper slap rail
38 Action stay
39 Metal standard
40 Pilot
41 Pilot wire
42 Key block
43 Key
44 Chase
45 Head
46 Key frame
47 Back rail
48 Balance rail
49 Front rail
50 Key bottom

In point of fact, however, the grand action suffers from the defect of its qualities. Erard introduced the repetition arm and made perfect repetition possible, the mechanical principle involved being that of counterpoise. And, while the weight of the grand hammer never interferes with the transference of power and individuality from the jack-head to the roller, the *complete* return of the hammer does cause an awkward upward jump to the key. It is this heavy return of the grand hammer and the kick it imparts to the key which makes pianists complain of the "heavy" touch of the grand piano. The keys of the grand piano are, of course, heavily loaded in the front balance to counteract the recoil of the hammer.

One suggestion to overcome this heavy return was to strengthen the resistance of the repetition lever by a second spring. Another invention was to have a spring flap, about three inches in length, beneath the end of the key, A third idea was a recoil pad on the wippen.

Most grands have a padded rail between the balance pins and the ivory tails of the keys, which helps to absorb the sudden and excessive upward movement of a key which has been heavily struck and immediately released.

[If arcs representing the line of movement of contacting parts are drawn from the various centres, it is possible to see how great would be the friction if the designer did not consider the relative speed of travel of the units comprising the section. It may be noted here that the efficiency of the bell-crank lever escapement is due, in part, to the fact that the fly moves at a much greater speed—about three times as great—than the bell-crank piece.]

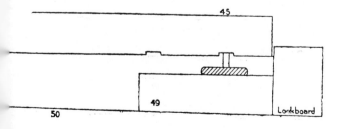

It is apposite to recall what is said about the exquisite performer, Chopin, who, when confronted with the Erard repetition action, preferred the heavy percussive touch of the old English direct-lever action.

The complaint is made to-day in some quarters that in any action embodying the Erard principle, the independence of the two units of each section (see Figs. 36 and 37, p. 80) causes a looseness and elusiveness of touch which is objectionable and which is not found in the English direct-lever action.

The upright action has no certain repetition unless there is the completed or almost completed return to rest of the key. The jack-head has to get under the notch before a new blow is possible. Recoil in the upright depends on the recoil angle of the shank, and very frequently upon springs. Fig. 39 shows a returning spring entering the butt at B, and in some actions a further spring is found between the damper slap-rail (see point 37 in Fig. 41) and the shank.

Fig. 41 (p. 84), which shows a unit of an underdamper upright action made by Messrs. Herrburger-Brooks of London, illustrates the movement of the respective parts of the action.

It is general to so construct actions that when set up in the piano, the jack-lever at rest (23, Fig. 41) is as much below the horizontal as it is above when the key is fully depressed.

Fig. 41 shows two arcs which indicate the path described by point 24 (the lever-bottom) and point 40 (the pilot-head) during the depression of a key.

COMPOUND ESCAPEMENT UPRIGHT ACTIONS.

If it is true that the grand action is very nearly perfect, it is also true that the action of the upright piano is far from perfect. The records in the Patents Office will furnish many examples of attempts to construct *upright* actions with an escapement lever.

A striking example is contained in the British patent No. 123,195: 1919 (granted to E. Brooks and K. Roberts). Fig. 42 shows a unit of the suggested design. The essential idea of the patent is the introduction of a balance or repetition arm, and this compares very well with the lever of the grand. It is claimed that this arm (which is provided with an escapement: note button 26 fastened to rail 22) ensures that the slightest

release of pressure on the key enables the fly to clear itself and
to be ready for another attack on the butt-notch.

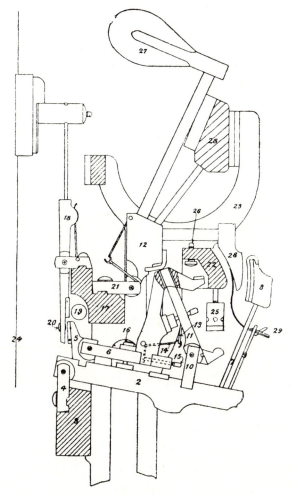

Figure 42

EXPLANATION OF FIG. 42.—Depression of the key raises the lever (2), in
which is centred the jack (11). Upon further depression of the key, the front
portion of the jack (11) comes into contact with a regulating button (25) in
the pin rail (22), which in turn rotates the jack clockwise about its centre,
giving it the necessary movement to clear the notch (12) and allowing the
butt to come into check. At the same time that this movement is taking

place, the balance or repetition lever is attacked by a screw button (26), which has the effect of retaining the lever in such a position that it supports the butt, leaving the jack-head free.

Normally, the notch is always resting on the jack-head, and the leather is thus always under compression. The function of the hammer rest (28) is not, in this design, to carry any weight from the hammer: it has no duty as a "rest," being used simply as a means of reducing the path of travel of the hammers when the "soft" (i.e., half-blow) pedal is depressed. It is claimed that the objectionable feeling of looseness during the early part of the key's movement (when the soft pedal is down) is absent in an upright piano fitted with this action. In other words, there is no lost motion; the spring (14) maintaining a contact between jack-head (11) and butt-notch (12), although the latter has been rotated from its centre on the fixture 21.

Lost Motion Attachments.

In an earlier chapter, it has been pointed out that the type of soft pedal which reduces the path of the hammer is not popular (in Europe, at any rate) for the horizontal form of piano; and for the upright, this reduction of the hammer-blow leaves much to be desired.

With the growing popularity of player and reproducing grand pianos, the shifting keyboard is not so desirable as heretofore. It is always a problem, if the action units are moved by the left pedal out of alignment with the pneumatic player units. It seems likely, therefore, that a lifting hammer-rail, which will permit the hammers to be lifted half-way to the strings. will in future be used for grand pianos. Yet the half-blow rail has the great failing that it creates lost motion. Also, the keys are apt to dip in front: a most annoying thing both to the eye and to the hand.

There has recently been patented by the Staib-Abendschein Co. of New York, a form of grand action which entirely eliminates the lost motion created by the movement of a hammer-lifting rail. Through the courtesy of the patentees, we are able to reproduce an illustration showing a unit of the design. Fig. 43 shows the hammer lifted half-way to the strings.

The raising of the action mechanism by a pedal must, in the normal types of actions, create a space between the fly and the notch, which space does seriously interfere with a fine execution by the performer. If the keys have a forward balance, they will dip to the front. A lesser key-movement might seem correct, seeing that the hammer, when the left-side pedal is in use, only travels half its full distance.

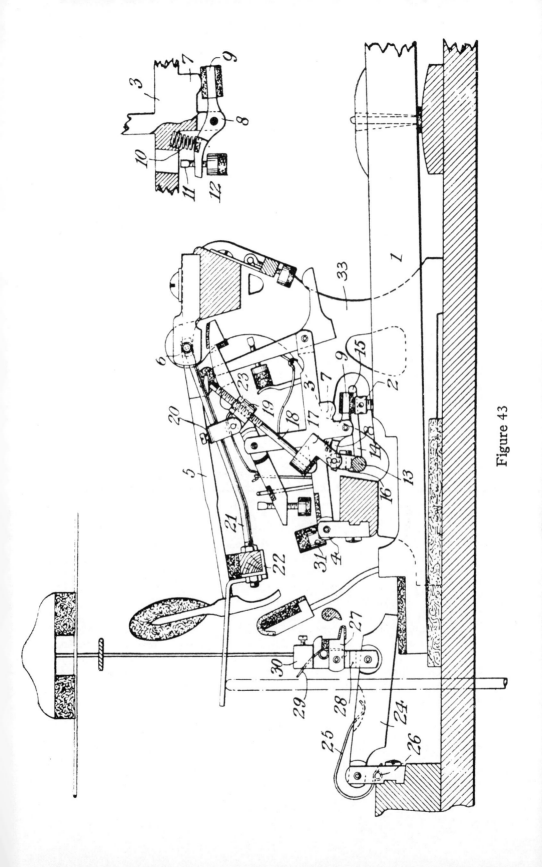

Figure 43

A 9 mm. touch coincides with a 5 cm. blow (⅜in. touch to 2in. blow). It is not practical to devise a 4 or 5 mm. touch (³⁄₁₆in.) for the half-blow movement. Skilled performers prefer the keys to have the same depth of depression, regardless of the conditions which are established in the action itself.

One suggestion made for avoiding lost motion was to fix the back rail of the key-frame on a centre, the left-side pedal raising the keys half the normal distance. There would be no space between the jacks and the butts, but the keys would, of course, dip at the front.

EXPLANATION OF FIG. 43.—The hammer is shown in an intermediate position, the soft pedal being depressed. 1 represents a key, 2 the capstan screw, and 3 the wippen pivoted at 4, and operating when raised by the key to throw the hammer 5, pivoted in the line 6. To a projection 7 on the under-side of the wippen 3, is pivoted a lever 8 (see the separate illustration), and the parts are so constructed that the forward end 9 of this lever is normally in contact with the projection 7 and the capstan screw 2. A spiral spring 10 is interposed between the rear arm of lever 8 and the wippen 3. The rear end of the lever 8 carries an adjusting screw 11 having a button 12 which rests in light contact with a lifter or lost motion rod 13. This rod 13 is supported by arms 14, and is secured to a bracket 16 to which is pivotally connected a connection block 17.

When the soft pedal is not in use, any movement of a key 1 is imparted directly by the capstan screw 2 through the padded end of the lever 8 to the wippen 3. By the action of the spiral spring 10 the lever 8 is held against the wippen at all times and the lever has no motion of its own. It is therefore, in effect, an integral part of the wippen, and its presence is not detectable by the player.

Assume, however, that the soft pedal be depressed. The rod 13 is raised and hence the button 12, and the rear end of the pivoted lever 8. The forward end of the lever is not thereby raised from the capstan screw 2, so that the rear end of the lever resting on the raised rod 13 becomes the power; the pivotal point of connection of the said lever 8, with the wippen the weight, and the forward end resting on the capstan screw 2 becomes the fulcrum.

When the key is depressed, however, and the capstan screw raises the *forward* end of the lever 8, the point of attack of this screw 2 upon the lever becomes the power, the pivotal connection of the lever with the wippen becomes the weight (which is still further raised), and the end resting upon the rod 13 becomes the fulcrum.

Fig. 44 shows a design for upright actions which provides the half-blow movement with the added advantage that there is no

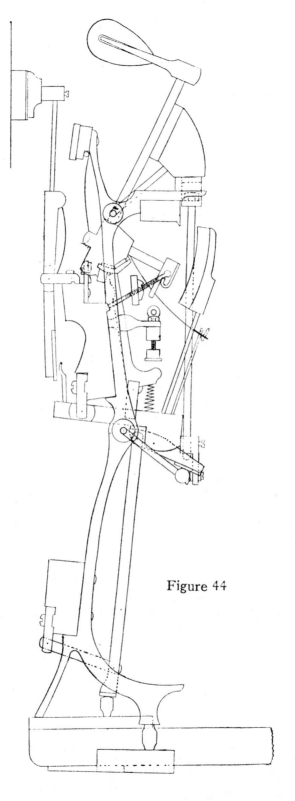

Figure 44

lost motion whatsoever. A compensating lever is introduced, and, as a glance at the figure will prove, when the hammer rail moves forward, so also does the jack lever and the jack move upward. Contact is maintained between key and prolonge and between jack head and fly.

THE SOSTENUTO ATTACHMENT.

The attachment to an action whereby an individual note may be sustained by a third pedal, irrespective of the position of the front end of the key is illustrated in Fig. 43 (page 89). Point 26 represents the damper-lever flange; 24 the lever; 25 a returning spring (mounted on the flange). The felted catch-block 27 is pivoted to the upright 28. The spring 29 holds the sostenuto mechanism in its uppermost position. Depression of the additional pedal actuates a catch rod, which holds the catch-block 27 and prevents the damper-rod and damper-head from falling on the vibrating string. When the third pedal is used, it is only those notes which the fingers of the performer have fully depressed and not released that are caught and held.

Complaint has been made that the sostenuto, or third pedal, has the fault that keys put down after the pedal is in use are tripped. This tripping is certainly very uncomfortable. For *upright* pianos, however, Herrburger of Paris designed some years ago a sostenuto attachment, the arrangement of which prevents any tripping to those keys struck after the middle pedal is employed. The unit is shown in Fig. 45 (page 93). The drawing explains itself: a moving rail, actuated by the pedal, throws out for each of the action units a small hardwood finger, which meets and holds the extended arm of the damper. The arrangement of the finger is such that a key struck when the sostenuto pedal is in use, does not meet any increase of resistance due to the lifting of the damper. The small spring which maintains the finger ready to catch the damper arm is very weak, and the damper moves off the string because the finger turns on its centre; the damper arm tail pushing the finger forward without any noticeable resistance to the fingers of the performer. Nearly every high-grade piano made both in Canada and America is fitted with a middle pedal. In England, the third pedal seems to be regarded as a curiosity.

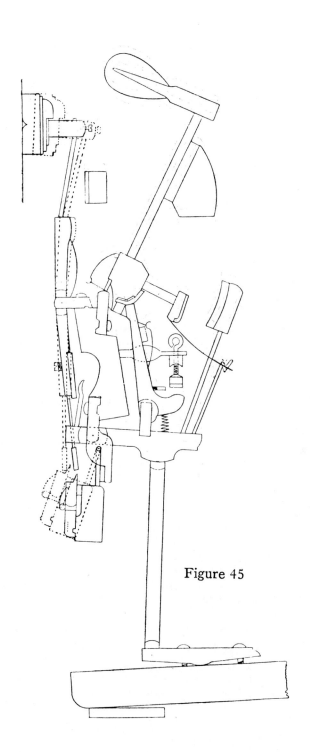

Figure 45

Setting up the Action.

In grand pianos, the return of the hammer to its position of rest is secured by the horizontal position of the action. The gravity of the hammer is more than sufficient for the purpose of recoil: and it is considered good practice to allow the hammer, as it meets the string, to overpass the horizontal position by 4 or 5 mm. This enables the action to be easily withdrawn and re-placed, there being more room between the underside of the wrest plank and the set-off screw of the escapement lever. If a hammer is put up to the vertical, it would not fall back at all. Every in-crement of approach to the vertical from the horizontal has its share in the reduction of recoil. However, this is of smaller moment than the other advantages gained by allowing the ham-mer to overpass the horizontal,— viz., the hammer-shank centre needs to be lower than it would be were the hammer at the time of blow at or below the horizontal.

The front loading of grand keys is, of course, imposed by the heavy weight of the action and hammer, though this loading can be avoided by inserting individual springs to carry part of the weight of the action sections.

Action makers draw the action with a definite length for the path of the hammer, usually 5 cm., and state the best position for the shank as it meets the string. A grand shank, as its hammer contacts with the string, could be either short or above the hori-zontal, just as the upright action shank is short of being parallel to the vertical. This overhang is called "rake," a word meaning angle.[16]

There are certain expressions in use which are universally accepted by all who are concerned with actions and the fitting of actions to pianos. The more essential words and phrases may be detailed thus :—

Strike (not to be confused with strike-line or strike-proportion). —The "strike" of an upright instrument is the measurement from the key-bottom surface to a point immediately beneath the extreme end of the treble bridge at the highest treble note. The strike fixes the height at which the key-bottom is to be left by the fitter-up: this because the strike is a total of the height of the action and the key. A moment's consideration will show that the strike for the upright piano can be as short as the bare work-

---

[16] The word "rake" is not peculiar to the piano-maker's vocabulary : it is frequently used to denote a backward inclination. A steamboat's funnels are said to be "raked." Rake is a deviation from truth.

ing space for the standard size of key and action. For example:

Surface of key-bottom to working centre of action lever, *say*	$1\frac{3}{4}$
Centre of lever to butt centre	$3\frac{1}{4}$
Butt centre to centre of hammer-wood	$5\frac{1}{8}$
inches	$10\frac{1}{8}$

In such an instance as this, the pilot screw, which would enter the key, would immediately attack the lever block. On the other hand, the strike of some pianos—and especially player-pianos—can be anything from fourteen to even eighteen inches.

The strike for a grand piano is by no means such a flexible factor as that of the upright.

Fig. 46 shows the two essential measurements. T C is the distance from key-bottom to plank, and T S is the distance from key-bottom to the string.

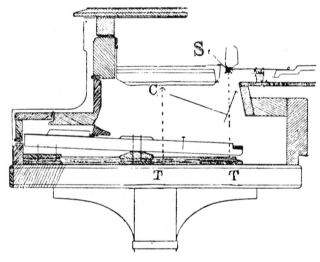

Figure 46

Fig. 32 (on page 75) shows the Schwander B unit. This is a very beautiful action.

The height from the keybottom surface to the underside of the wrest plank in the set-up of this action needs to be $6\frac{1}{4}$ inches. The total distance from keybed to string would be 8 inches. The distance from keybed to the primary working centre of wippen is $3\frac{1}{4}$ inches. The blow is 2 inches, touch 10 millimetres, and the key balance ratio 10 inches $\times$ $5\frac{1}{8}$ inches. The Schwander C action allows 6 inches between keybed and wrest plank.

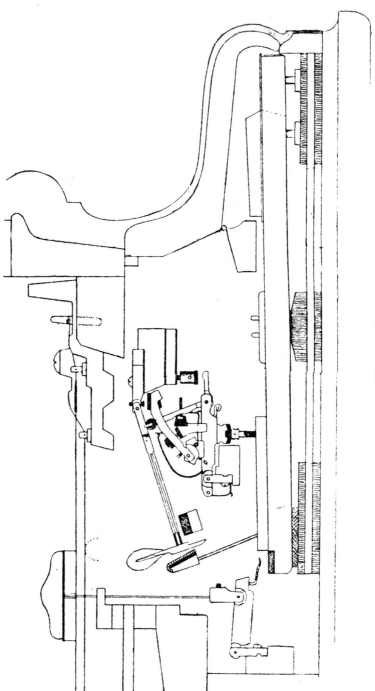

Figure 47

Fig. 47 shows another type of grand action, set up in the case. (The illustration is also interesting in regard to the arrangement of the upper-bearing levels.)

Keybottom Measurement.—This is taken from the inside of the lock rail to the surface of the steel strings. It is generally about 17 inches. The minimum distance allowable between the dead end of the key and the surface of the extreme bass string is about half-an-inch.

Blow.—This represents the path through which the hammer travels, and is intended to be 5 cm., which approximates to 2 inches. Blow is measured in a horizontal line. (The piano finisher tests with a small piece of wood called the blow-piece, which is inserted between the hammer nose and the string.) The actual movement of the hammer is curved, as it represents the arc of a circle of 13·9 cm. radius, and is therefore a little more than 2 inches. Figure 48 illustrates this point.

Touch.—This is the degree to which the front end of the key is capable of depression. Perhaps this degree of depression should be called "depth of touch," because an artist by "touch" understands that sensitive feeling imparted to the finger by the collective movement of the key and the action parts.

Key Balance Ratio.—The fulcrum point of the piano key is calculated not merely from the vertical rise of the action lever. The loss by circular motion at the pilot-head must be considered. Action makers state what they consider to be the correct proportion for balance and back length of key.

Rake.—The angle which the hammer shank as it meets the string makes with the vertical (or horizontal) is the rake. An action fitted with butt-returning springs (such as is shown in Fig. 48) does not require so much overhang as does the action which depends on gravity alone for the recoil of the hammer. A minimum rake of 4.5 mm., measured on the 13 cm. line, which is the length of shank, gives an angle of 2°.

It is more general to find a rake of $\frac{5}{16}$ or $\frac{3}{8}$, giving 3° overhang. The procedure in some factories is to use a rake-block or template, while others prefer to take the distances from a square projected against the ends of the piano case.

The recoil of the hammer is sometimes assisted by the fact that the butt-centre is not in a direct line with the shank centre. A glance at Fig. 48 shows this centre to be sensibly nearer to the strings. As the power is from the butt centre to the centre of the shank, it would seem that, if the butts were bored direct to the turning centre, a better blow would result. Whether the reason is economy of material or merely complying with a fixed rule dictated by custom, most butts are bored so that the turning point is about 4 mm. nearer to the strings than the shank centre line.

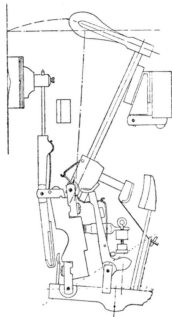

Figure 48

It is a fact that in practice the angle varies with the caprice and knowledge of the workman. The designer of the upright action usually ignores the angle which the steel strings sometimes make with the vertical, and works from a line drawn perpendicularly through the strike point.

It is assumed that the steel strings of the grand run horizontally. The hammers are put on the shank by the grand finisher, and the head is generally at right angles to the shank line, both for the bass and also the treble sections. (The finisher of the upright piano is, of course, supplied with the shank and head complete.)

　　　　.　　　　.　　　　.　　　　.　　　　.

The exact regulation of the units of the action, when it is set up in the piano, is outside the sphere of the written word. The practical execution of "laying the keys" and "regulating the action" is the craft of the workman known as the "piano finisher." It is a highly-specialised craft," and is, in the result, subdivided, for the regulation of a horizontal piano is the work of the "grand finisher."

Most finishers give a greater "set-off" than is necessary. In modern actions, the danger of blocking is very small; moreover, there is no part of the action regulation which suffers less from atmospheric changes than the set-off device. A moment's thought shows that if the hammer travel is 2in. and $\frac{1}{8}$in. set-off is given, there is a loss of power of over six per cent. A $\frac{1}{16}$in. set-off is adequate.

Check felt will swell when damp, and in upright actions blocking occurs through the balance hammer being again forced forward by the after-touch. Some allowance should always be given to guard against this.

Fig. 49 (on p. 100) shows a section of an upright action. This drawing was published by an American action manufacturer (F. H. Abendschein) in an attempt to standardise action brackets and certain features of action construction. It is interesting in that it shows a method of working general in the United States. The quotation (on p. 101) explains the set-up of the action in the piano.

In considering the setting up of the upright action, it would be well to emphasize the paramount importance of hammer recoil. The choice of wood for the shanks is important. One of the reasons which dictate the use of hickory or maple is that these woods have a low flexibility but a high elasticity. A direct blow, without any tendency to "slew," is necessary. It is then imperative that the hammer recoils rapidly. Now, the recoil is not instantaneous, for whenever motion is reversed by impact, as in the case of a felt-covered hammer hitting a tensioned steel wire, there is a period of time during which the moving object is in contact with that from which it rebounds. Further, this lag—this period of rest—may be long or short, and is affected by the elasticity of both objects. When the hammer is driven forward to the string, if the shank is *flexible*, there is a bowing action,[17] the nose has a stroking action upon the wire, with objectionable

---

[17] As an example of this, the last few treble hammers of old pianos fitted with "sticker" actions may be mentioned. If the hammers are pressed gently with the fingers against the strings, it is found that they are appreciably distant from the pins of the old-time plank bridge. Yet upon examination the faces of the hammers are found to be deeply cut. The bowing action of the cedar-wood shanks is thereby proved.

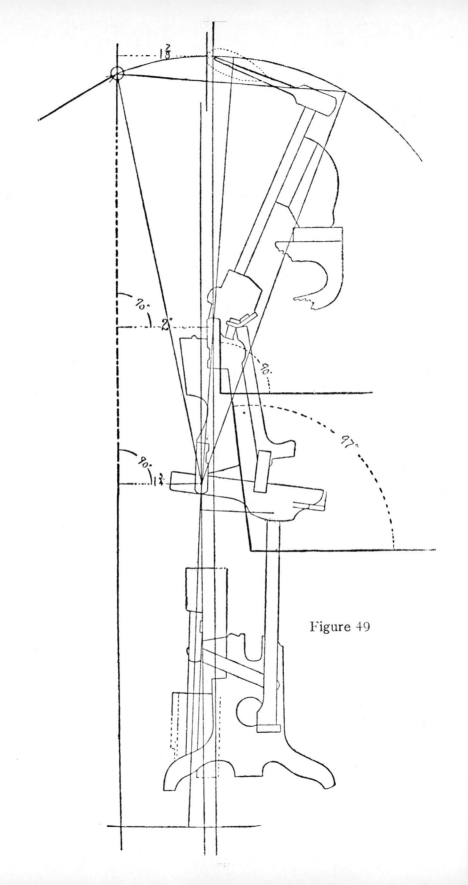

Figure 49

results to the ultimate tone. From which it is to be seen that a wood of small flexibility is desirable. Flexibility in stems means bending in the act of striking the wires. There is bound to be some bending, and this brings in the different and further factor of elasticity. The less the bending the better: but what the shank does bend, it is of importance to recover rapidly. The longer the contact, the more the hammer ceases to be a string agitator and becomes a damper, thereby destroying its own work.

EXPLANATION OF FIGURE 49.

"The three most important centres of this action are the butt, wip and fly, The distance between the butt and wip is 3¼ inches. The drawing shows that the wip is ¼ inch nearer the strings than the butt centre. The velocity diagram automatically works out that distance. When the action is set so that the wip centre is ¼ inch to the rear of the butt centre, this permits the front of the action rail to assume an angle of 97 degrees. This insures a maximum efficiency of the action movement. With this setting, the face of the butt flange stands at an angle of 90 degrees. All these angles are reckoned from the bed, which is assumed to be horizontal. The blow-distance is 1⅞ inches. The correct distance is 2 inches, but an allowance of ⅛ inch is made for the wear on the face of the hammer. The distance between the butt centre and striking point should be 5⅝ inches."

HISTORICAL.

It is said by some that the story of music during the past two centuries has largely been the history of the piano. Piano history commences with the introduction, in 1709, by the Paduan harpsichord maker (Cristofori) of a *hammer action*. The piano combines the sustained tone of the clavichord with the power of the harpsichord, because it has heavier strings and because it possesses a hammer action. The action of Cristofori was the work of a mechanical genius. It permitted the jack to "escape," an individual damper was provided for each note, and a check *(paramartello)* was added.

The outstanding dates in the history of the piano are 1709, 1821 and 1826. For a hundred years there has been no far-reaching improvement: there have been improvements in details only.

In 1821, Sebastian Erard,[18] a French national, was granted protection for a "repetition grand check action."

[18] The house of Erard established a factory in England early in the nineteenth century, near by Great Marlborough Street, London, W. It is known that Sebastian Erard first came to England in 1786. The house of Erard is to-day known as S. & P. Erard, after Sebastian and his nephew Pierre. The Paris factory was established in 1780, and the London agency in 1792. Erards made pianos in London for some seventy years, first in Great Marlborough Street (where offices and show-rooms are still maintained), and later at Warwick Road, Kensington.

In 1826, Robert Wornum, an Englishman, was granted protection for "certain improvements in pianofortes......which relate entirely to the action." The grand action of to-day is substantially as that first patented by Erard. The action of the upright piano of this day is built exactly on the principles laid down by Wornum. In neither instance has any essential feature been added or eliminated. The house of Erard is still to be numbered with the really great piano houses of the world. How unfortunate that the name of Wornum is confined to a few very old pianos.

By the invention of the piano action, the harpsichord was changed into an instrument of *percussion*. Dr. Rimbault, in the following words, details how the "scratch with a sound at the end of it" was doomed to a lingering fate: the piano was born.

> *The quill, pig's bristle, thorn, ivory tongue, leathern tongue &c., were soon to be banished. A small hammer was made to strike the string and evoke a clear, precise, and delicate tonr... The "scratch with a sound at the end of it" was doomed.*

The first Cristofori action (1707 or 1709) permitted an escapement. The interlocked silken cord (Fig. 50) served to facilitate repetition.

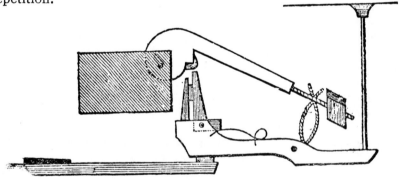

Figure 50

In Fig. 51 the later form of the Cristofori design is shown, and it will be seen that a rigid back check for catching the hammer replaced the cord.

It may be said that in its final form (1720) this action includes all the requirements of a modern pianoforte action. The Italian harpsichord was shallow in construction, and Cristofori in his pianos imitated this form. His action had to conform to the shallow case work. It will be observed that he was obliged to pierce the key with the hopper.

The hammer of the earlier model was a small wooden block covered with leather.

Cristofori died in 1731, at the age of forty-eight. For many years prior to his death, he enjoyed, according to one writer, the sybaritic court life of the Grand Duke of Tuscany, to which nobleman he was musical instrument maker. Another suggestion was that he hastened his end by allowing his genius to drive him to over exertion.

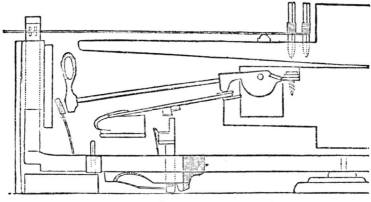

Figure 51

It is a remarkable coincidence that an Italian, a German, and a Frenchman, all within a few years, should each conceive the idea of the *piano-e-forte*. Sir George Grove's Dictionary of Music concedes priority to Cristofori, but the work of the German Schröter, and the Parisian Marius deserves some consideration.

Marius in 1716 submitted three models of *harpsichord hammer actions* (*clavecin à maillets*) to the Royal Academy of Sciences: one of these was a downward-striking hammer action.

Christopher Gottlieb Schröter was born at Hohenstein in 1699. In 1717 he constructed his "clavier with *hammers*." This action has been described as a model of innocent simplicity. Schröter declared that he conceived the idea of a hammer action after watching the virtuoso Hebenstreit perform on his monster *Hackbrett* (dulcimer). The Schröter design is undoubtedly the fundamental of the German and Vienna actions.

Gottfried Silbermann, the organ builder and clavichord maker of Dresden, has been called the father of the German pianoforte industry. Records disclose that he was also a very shrewd business man, for when the great Bach condemned in unmeasured terms Silbermann's own action, Silbermann copied the Cristofori design, and eventually induced Bach to approve the new instrument. He also improved the Schröter action.

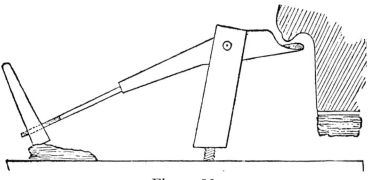

Figure 52

Gottfried was born in Saxony in 1683, served an apprenticeship as a cabinet-maker, then followed the example of his talented elder brother, Andreas Silbermann, and took to organ building.

Gottfried was working at Freiburg about 1712 upon a church organ, but he had a great weakness for the gentler sex, and, being continually involved in serious affairs, had to flee to his brother at Strasburg. Here he was found endeavouring to escape with a nun, and again had to leave hurriedly. Silbermann is the romantic figure of the early pianoforte industry. Withal, he was a fine mechanic. His first action design (1728) is shown in Fig. 52. He died in 1756. During his life, he erected many large organs.

Johann Andreas Stein was a pupil of Silbermann, and learned piano making in Silbermann's workshops. He was established at Augsburg about 1754: and it was Stein who invented the "hopper action," which prevented the blocking of the hammers on the strings. Stein's pianos were copied everywhere, but more particularly by the Vienna makers, and Stein is entitled to be called the Father of the Viennese school. After his death at Augsburg in 1792, his daughter Nannette left Saxony for Vienna. In addition to being an able pianist, Nannette was a practical piano maker, and could tune her own instruments. She married, in

1793, Andreas Streicher, and together they developed the Viennese action. Beethoven, when at Bonn, is known to have had a decided liking for the Stein piano. The Streicher Viennese action is shown in Fig. 53 : *a* is the key, *b* the hopper, *i* the hopper spring; *l* is the standard in which the hammer-butt *d* is centred; the set-off button is *h*, the check *f*, and the damper *g*.

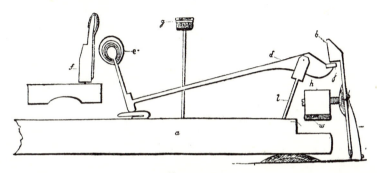

Figure 53

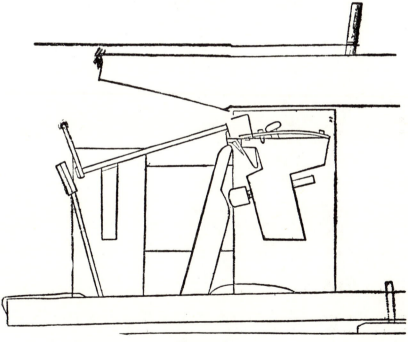

Figure 54

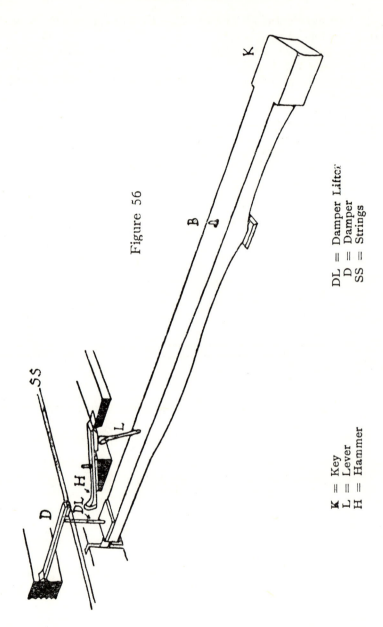

Figure 56

K = Key
L = Lever
H = Hammer

DL = Damper Lifter
D = Damper
SS = Strings

The Seven Years' War (1755-1762) did considerable harm to the small industry of piano making in Saxony. The country was devastated and the workmen scattered, many coming to England. An old workshop tradition—the tale of the Twelve Apostles—owes its origin to this fact. Zumpe, Backers, Geib, and others, started a new industry in London.

The first piano brought into England had been made, it is assumed, by an English monk at Rome, Father Wood. It followed the Cristofori model. The new instrument made little progress until after the Seven Years' War. Two workers, both pupils of Silbermann, Johannes Zumpe and Americus Backers, were then established in London. Backers brought out what will always be known as the English action: it is shown in Fig. 54.

We must digress for a moment to consider Fig. 55. Here we have the Broadwood grand direct-lever action. Hipkins has dated this model 1895. Backers's action is dated 1776. As a glance will prove, there is no essential difference: both are single escapement units.

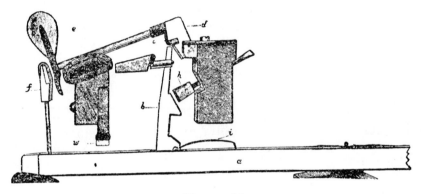

Figure 55

a = the key	e = hammer head
b = the hopper	f = check
c = notch	h = set off button and screw
d = butt	i = hopper returning spring

Fig. 56 shows the action of a square piano by Johannes Broadwood dated 1774. The drawing is reproduced through the courtesy of Messrs. Broadwood from a recent pamphlet on old instruments.

The earliest record in Broadwood's books is 1773: a Broadwood model.

John Broadwood first came to London from Scotland in 1732. Soon, in following his trade as a joiner, he found himself at the workshop of Burkat Shudi,[19] 33, Great Pulteney Street. Shudi was first a cabinet maker, but he had established himself as a harpsichord maker of some renown, having worked for a time with the Flemish harpsichord maker, Tabel. Broadwood married Shudi's daughter in 1769.

The Broadwood action shown in Fig. 56 is the "mop-stick" or "old man's head" type, which has the fault that there was no certain escapement. It will be remembered that the later Cristofori model had a sure escapement, and Backers (Fig. 54) introduced a very effective escapement.

But the merit of introducing the hopper jack and spring belongs to John Geib. Geib made pianos for Longman & Broderip, musical instrument dealers and music publishers, of Cheapside, which business merged, through Clementi, into the firm of Collard & Collard. Geib's action, patented in 1786, was known as the "grasshopper" action.

Broadwood placed the wrest plank of his pianos along the back of the case instead of along the right-hand side of the case as it always had been in the clavichord. And everywhere, even by the German school, this form was adopted. The construction of the modern grand has, of course, reverted to the Cristofori type, with the wrest plank above the keyboard and the hammer-rise at the end of the key (instead of towards the centre of the key, as in the Viennese action).

In 1821, the mechanical genius, Sebastian Erard, patented his double - escapement grand action. The original form is shown in Fig. 57. This action was a distinct departure from the Cristofori, Schröter and Backers actions. The depression of the piano key forced down the damper. It was an under-damper action.

The Revolution drove Erard to London. Erard was a man of extreme culture and refinement : and, just as he was in close contact with the French aristocracy, so also did he make influential friends with the English peers. His action patent led to the most unusual request for a patent renewal, and his friends succeeded in carrying sufficient support in the House of Lords to grant an extension for the double-escapement action.

---

[19] Shudi came from Switzerland, having been born at Schwanden in 1702. His original name was Burckhardt Tschudi. It was at 33, Great Pulteney Street, that Mozart practised on the harpsichord built by Shudi for Frederick, King of Prussia.

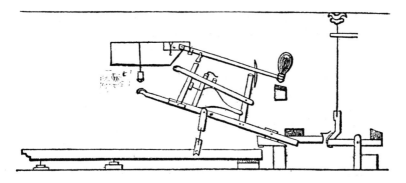

Figure 57

As has been pointed out earlier, "double escapement" is a misnomer, but Fig. 58, though illustrating an early form, will explain the operation of the unit. As the action is made and

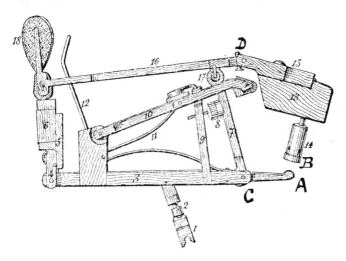

Figure 58

1 Lever pilot	10 Repetition arm
2 Double-thread screw	11 Double spring
3 Lever	12 Check wire
4 Lever flange	13 Action beam
5 Lever rail	14 Set-off button
6 Hammer rest	15 Hammer flange
7 Jack	16 Hammer flange
8 Jack button	17 Roller
9 Escapement button arm	18 Hammer

regulated to-day (and most likely this was the intention of the inventor), there is one escapement,—that is, when point A meets B. But the jack (7), being hinged at C, permits the transference of the utmost power and individuality, because, when the arm (10) meets D, there is direct contact between jack and roller: the hammer having been lifted by the arm (10), which arm, after the blow, cushions back the roller. The slightest release of pressure enables the jack to clear itself.

It will be noted that the checking was on the beam side of the hammer and against the check wire (12 in the drawing).

It would be a mistake to imagine that "double escapement" actions built on the Erard principle are popular with every maker.

Erard, it is recorded, at the age of thirteen years, climbed the Strasburg steeple (he was born at Strasburg in 1752) and sat upon the top of the cross, which was no mean exploit for one who has towered so supremely above all his contemporaries.

On the expiry of Erard's various patents, the actions were made in many factories: but Erard's continued the production of the action and its parts. Various firms bought the units and assembled them.

Henry Herz of Paris somewhat modified and simplified the Erard form. Collard also used a modification, introducing an additional lever. Mr. G. D. Rose of Broadwood's also introduced a modification. Pleyel, Wolff & Co., the French makers, likewise used a form peculiar to themselves. But the Erard principle is maintained in all forms of the "double escapement" grand action.

Two modern examples are shown in Fig. 59 (on page 111) and Fig. 32 (on page 75). The drawings also show the action standard. Fig. 59 shows an American adaptation, known as the Cambridge action.

Fig. 32 shows the Schwander B action, made by Herrburger Brooks, of London. The basis of this latter action as now manufactured is the wippen, which is shown enlarged, but in a slightly varied form, in Fig. 31 (on page 74). Its simplicity is at once apparent, as also — to the experienced eye — is the facility for regulation, the screw governing the strength of the single spring being readily accessible.

In contrast to these "double escapement" units, Fig. 60 shows the Brinsmead grand action,— a single escapement unit. This action (it was manufactured extensively up to a few years ago) gave a very easy and powerful stroke. It was, however, some-

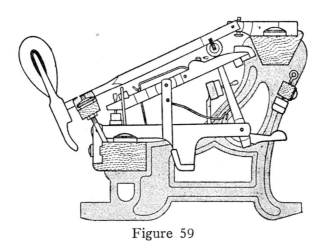

Figure 59

what liable to derangement and the wear was considerable; withal, this type has certain advantages, and consequently it has many supporters.

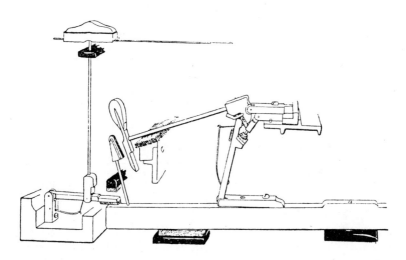

Figure 60

EARLY UPRIGHT ACTIONS.

As early as 1745, C. E. Friederici, of Gera, Germany (another pupil of Silbermann) constructed a *vertical* grand piano. The Friederici action is shown in Fig. 61.

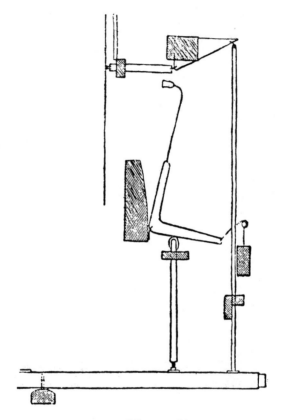

Figure 61

In 1780, J. Schmidt of Salzburg built an upright piano; yet it is generally accepted that J. I. Hawkins of Philadelphia was the pioneer of the upright piano.

John Isaac Hawkins was an Englishman living in America, and he patented this upright instrument in 1800, both in America and—under his father's name, Isaac Hawkins—in England. The

Patent is No. 2446/1800. No drawing accompanies the specification of the English patent.

The upright spinet and harpsichord were in reality horizontal instruments turned on edge, and usually placed upon a stand:

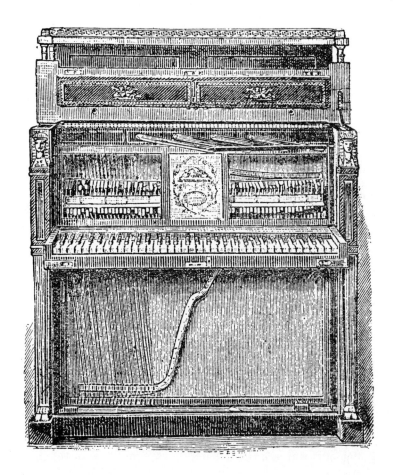

Figure 62

but the upright piano of Hawkins had strings descending below the keyboard, and the bottom of the instrument was on the floor. Fig. 62 shows the Hawkins upright.

The Broadwood collection of old instruments contains one of these Hawkins uprights, and a quotation from a Broadwood pamphlet is interesting :—

"A pianoforte made in 1800 by John Isaac Hawkins, who invented the modern upright piano. The disposition of the keyboard in relation to the strings, the complete iron frame, the independent sounding-board, mechanical tuning pins, equal tension scaling, and the mechanism upon modern lines, with metal supports, together present an astonishing example of inventions completely carried out half-a-century before their general adoption. The keyboard is arranged to fold up, as is now sometimes done in pianofortes for yachts. Only lack of experience and knowledge of the requirements of practical pianoforte construction appear to have prevented Hawkins from succeeding in his most promising experiments."

A further quotation from this same pamphlet[20] must be given, because it brings us to the next step in the development of the upright piano and its action.

"A cabinet pianoforte made by Broadwood in 1843. This type (the cabinet) was originated by Southwell in 1804. It was popular for over forty years, although in many respects the ideas upon which it was constructed were less advanced than those of Hawkins. Comparison of the action with that of Hawkins shows that it retains an earlier escapement. The Hawkins action, on the other hand, bears a great resemblance to the modern mechanism, though for half-a-century it was entirely forgotten."

The Southwell cabinet piano was fitted with the sticker action, which action, always popular with English makers, is prefigured in the Friederici action of 1745 (see Fig. 61), and was first patented by "William Southwell, musical instrument maker, of the City of Dublin" (Patent No. 3029 / 1807).

The Southwell cabinet pianos were frequently instruments of beautiful tone, though sometimes ungainly in structure. The fact that, as the last quotation proves, Broadwood's were making this type of piano as late as 1843 shows how popular it had become; and it is remarkable that the now obsolete sticker action of the cabinet piano should have held the field so long. Even down to 1880 there were English makers of some standing who preferred the Southwell hinged "sticker" action for their uprights. By this time, however, it had been fore-shortened and made more compact; yet it retained the earlier escapement, and the hammer had to carry with it both a lever and a sticker, the latter usually weighted with one or more discs of lead. Which meant that the hammer, before it could rebound, had to overcome the inertia of the weighted sticker. Further, the sticker action depended upon the pliability of vellum and leather for its movements.

[20] " The Broadwood Collection of Antique Instruments : Notes and Illustrations." To be obtained from John Broadwood & Sons, Ltd., 158 New Bond Street, London, W.

Fig. 63 shows the sticker action in its later form.

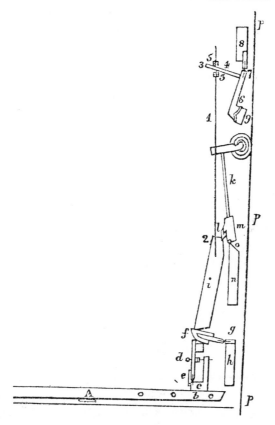

Figure 63

The key (A) pushes up the hopper (c). The regulating pin (d) and spring (e) determine the touch. The hopper is met by the lever (f), which by a hinge (g) is fastened to the lever rail (h). Above this is the sticker (i), to which the hammer (k) is hinged at (l) by a fastening of wash-leather. The butt (m) of the hammer being hinged to the hammer rail (n), in the point (o) it is obvious that the pressing down of the key (A) must drive up the sticker (i), and consequently cause the hammer (k) to strike against the string (ppp).

The damper wire (1) is fastened sideways into the sticker at (2), so as to pass upright between the butts (m). The top of the wire forms the screw (3), passing through the arm of the damper (4), which is secured to it by (5 5). The damper (6), which is fixed by a hinge (7) to the damper rail (8), being thus elevated with the sticker (i) raises its felt surface (9) off the string (ppp). Immediately upon the hand being taken off the key, the weight of the sticker (i) causes the wire to fall, stopping the vibration.

In 1821 William Southwell patented a design (No. 4546) for a checked-sticker action. Fig. 64 and the small type explanation here following are taken from the specification.

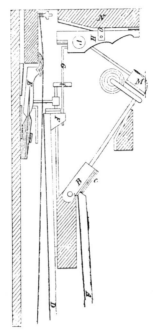

Figure 64

Letter *A*, marked on the plan or drawing, is a sticker, which can be taken off and put on in an instant, by means of a small screw and steady pin, which fixes it to the butt of the hammer at *B*, going through a small piece of wood at *C*, which piece of wood and the sticker *A* are connected together by a single leather joint. The said sticker *A* has at its upper end a small part left square, about the sixteenth part of an inch, which raises the hammer up with greater powers.

D is a back sticker, one quarter of an inch from the strings, and on the end is put leather to prevent noise in raising the damper *E*. At the same end is glued a block of wood *F* to receive a wire *G*, which is turned square at the upper end to raise the check lever *H*. The said wire works in a socket *I* to keep it steady.

When the key is put in motion, it raises the check lever *H*, and puts down the other end of the check *M*, and receives the end of the hammer after the stroke is given, which completely prevents the hammer from doubling or rebounding against the strings.

Notwithstanding the success of the Southwell sticker action, as used in the cabinet type of piano, we are confronted with the fact that the enduring popularity of the upright form was due very largely to the changes adopted by Robert Wornum, a London piano maker. Wornum made the upright a practical instrument.

In the little upright pianos first made by Wornum (from 1811 onwards), the action shown in Fig. 65 was used. The defects of this action are that there is no checking, and that the escapement is very poor, depending on a limitation of the key's movement, and the angle of the hopper (*b*).

a Key
b Hopper
c String
d Hammer rail
e Hammer
f Damper and wire
g Damper rail
h Ruler
ii Springs

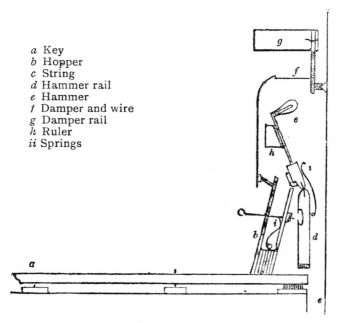

Figure 65

In 1811 Wornum had brought out a low upright (3ft. 3in.), with diagonal strings. This piano had five-and-a-half octaves and widely extended ends to accommodate the extra length of string due to diagonal scaling. Another (and strange) feature of this instrument was that, when access to the strings was necessary, all one had to do was to touch a small latch, when both action and keys could be swung on one side, like the opening of a door. In 1813 Wornum constructed a small upright (about 3ft. 6in.), with vertical strings.

Later, Wornum used an action to which a check and balance

hammer were added.   One form of this check action is shown in Fig. 66.

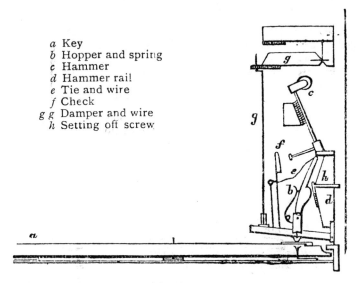

a Key
b Hopper and spring
c Hammer
d Hammer rail
e Tie and wire
f Check
g g Damper and wire
h Setting off screw

Figure 66

The tie or tape prevented the undue separation of the two parts of each unit.   Escapement in this action was made possible by the bulging design of the hopper, which, as it met the inclined face of the hammer rail, forced the fly from under the notch and prevented blocking.   The bell-crank lever escapement of to-day (see Fig. 33, page 75) has at times been credited to Wornum, but this is not correct, for Erard in his 1821 grand action patent invented this form of "setting off," and early in the last century Erard's employed the same idea in their upright actions.

The principle is that of a small depth of "after touch" which continues the movement of the jack, while contact is made with some rigid fixture, thus forcing out the jack from the notch.   In the Erard grand action, a bell-crank piece is added to the jack lever, which meets the padded underface of a rigid button, the jack-fly rotating clockwise on the "secondary centre" of the jack-lever.   (See Fig. 58, page 109.)

Fig. 66 shows that the Wornum escapement was capable of a fine adjustment.   (See set-off screw h, which pierces the hammer rail d.)   The rail d had a strip of cloth on its inclined face.   If an examination is made of the Backers grand action of 1776 (see

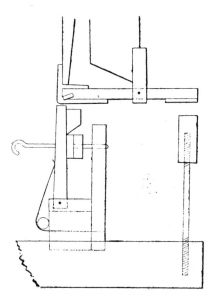

Figure 68
(Illustration taken from the Wornum Patent, No. 5678, 1828)

Fig. 54, page 105),, it will be seen that the two escapements—
Backers' and Wornum's—are very similar.

The later Wornum actions were centred with a cloth bushing,
which gave a ready response, precision and durability, and the
addition of the check and tie gave accurate repetition.

The following directions, which must be familiar to many
tuners, are to be found on the ruler (or hammer rail) of Wornum's pianos :—

*Directions for the New Piccolo, Harmonic, and Cabinet Piano-Fortes, with
Patent Double Action.*

*Invented and Manufactured by Robert Wornum, at the Music Hall,
Store Street, Bedford Square.*

To put on a String, take out the Action.— To set the Hammers off, draw the
Action forward at top, and with a small screw driver, turn the hopper screws
at the back of the hammer rail.—To set the hoppers up to the butts, turn the
screws in the Keys ; observing, always to leave a space the thickness of a
card, between the hopper and the butt.—To regulate the ties, bend their wires
back or forward, as may be requisite ; observing always to leave the tie a
little slack.— To regulate the Checks, bend the wires till the Hammer falls
nearly to the Ruler. These directions are given as matters of information ;
but from the great stability of this Action, they are not likely to be needed.

c Socket
d Hammer
e Hammer ruler
f Hammer rail
g Sticker
i Damper wire and button
h Check lever
j Check
k k Hopper centre and mortoise
     bushed
   l Hopper spring fixed to sticker
   m Dog spring fixed in hopper
     to keep the hammer from
     dancing after the blow.
   n Lifting wire for check fixed
     in sticker with worm and
     slipped into check lever ;
     hole bushed.

The novelties of the *double* action are a *double* hammer rail, to which are fixed both hammers and hoppers ; the butt or lever of the hopper is centred to the lower part of this rail, and the regulating pin passes through the hopper mortoise in the middle part of it.

In the sticker is fixed a bent wire (*n*) for lifting the check lever ; the end connected with the sticker is tapped, and a hole being drilled, it is pressed in at the left side ; the other end is put into a bushed hole in the check lever.

From the right side of the hopper a spring, called a dog, is projected, and passes to the front at the lower part of the hammer shank, by which the hammer is prevented from dancing after the hand is off the key.

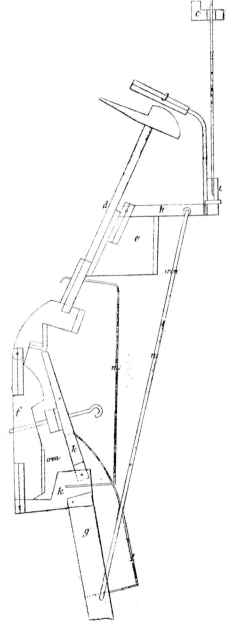

Figure 67
(Taken from the Wornum Patent, No. 5384, 1826)

The idea of checking the *upright* hammer head itself has never been successful, though Cristofori, of course, successfully checked the grand hammer with a check-piece mounted on the tail of the key. (See Fig. 51, page 103.)

The form of checking which Robert Wornum introduced in his 1826 patent (No. 5384) was probably suggested by the grand action; Wornum tried to check the upright hammer *head* with a check piece, as will be seen from Fig. 67, which is taken from the specification.

In 1828 Wornum patented an entirely different form of checking, which is illustrated in Fig. 68 on page 119 (from Patent No. 5678). The quotation from the specification explains the working:

> The novelty is applied to the lever and the key, and effects a check to the hammer when in action. The lever is longer than usual and is employed at both ends. The (extra) work which is affixed to the key consists of a wire and a button, the wire screwed into the key at the end and the button screwed on the top of the wire. Its use is to press against the back or tail of the lever after every blow given to the front by the hopper, thereby effecting a most simple and perfect check against unnecessary motion in the hammer, which is a great defect in all single actions.

The Wornum tape-check design illustrated in Fig. 66 is, however, the only one which endured; it is, in fact, the prototype of all modern upright forms.

Pleyel and Pape of Paris took the Wornum action and achieved considerable results in improvements. The action was made in Paris in large numbers; and the product was of such uniform and excellent quality that piano makers, both in Germany and England, announced that they embodied "French" (Paris made) actions in their pianos. It was thus that the action of the Englishman Robert Wornum came to be called the French or Pleyel action. The Paris makers, curiously enough, called the action *mécanique anglaise*.

An action design which is entirely peculiar to itself, and which from a commercial point of view at any rate, was very successful must be mentioned,—it is the Molineux spring and loop action. Fig. 69 is taken from the first Molineux patent (No. 2509, 1862). Molineux was a Manchester joiner, born in 1802 and dying in London in 1891.

There were many minor alterations in this spring and loop action, and its popularity continued down to a few years ago. The wear in these actions was extraordinary heavy, the check leather and the balance hammer coverings being very often ground away to powder. Inasmuch as the point of contact of the checking was very much nearer the working centre, regula-

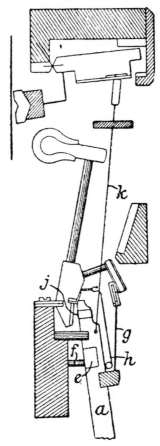

Figure 69

The lower end of the sticker *a* rests on a piece of felt covering an adjusting-screw in the key, and is connected by a double jointed piece to a fixed rail. The upper end carries a check *g*, a spring *h*, a damper wire *k*, and an adjusting screw *j*. The sticker is guided by the pin *f* in the slot *e*. The screw *j* is adjusted so that the sticker is pushed off the butt as the hammer strikes the string.

tion was never very easy after a little use had worn the con‑ tact surfaces. The shaped check of the modern tape check action is much farther away, at the moment of contact, from the‑ working centre than was the case with the Molineux design.

The tape check design gives a better touch with less wear together with a more even attack, and the original tape check

action is to be seen in the Wornum form shown in Fig. 66
(page 118).

The extent to which the Wornum design has been developed
may be gauged by the following illustrations.

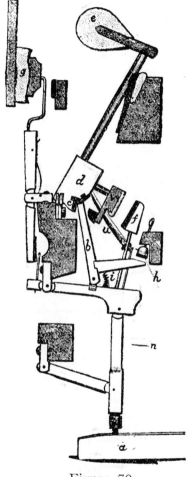

Figure 70

Fig. 70 shows a Broadwood design, in which *a* is the key,
b the hopper, *c* the notch, *d* the hammer butt, in which is inserted
the shank of *e*, the hammer-head; *f* is the check, *g* the damper.
h the set-off button held rigid by a rail extending the length of
the action. Now, *i* shows the hopper spring, which in this unit is

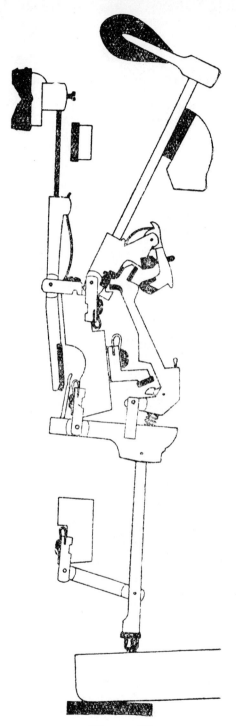

Figure 72

a spiral spring, and was the invention of a very capable piano maker of Paris, A. Bord. The tape *u* is, of course, the invention of Wornum.

Fig. 71 shows an American adaptation, in which the checking is on the outside of the set-off rail (which is, of course, more general), and not on the beam side, as in the Broadwood design in Fig. 70.

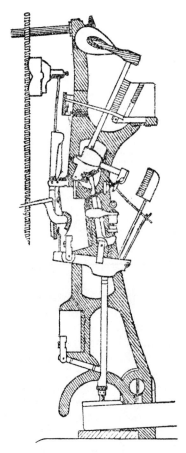

Figure 71

Fig. 72 shows an American form made by Staib-Abendschein in which the jack and hopper are of somewhat unique design.

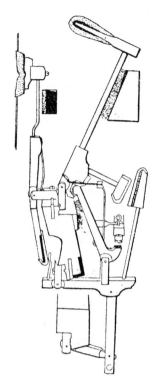

Figure 73

In Fig. 73 we have a design embodying the Brinsmead patents. The position of the recoil spring is interesting, also the absence of a jack spiral spring: which raises an important point. Is repetition in the upright action influenced more by the rapid recoil of the hammer and the prevention of undue separation of hammer and wippen units of the section, or is it rather a matter of designing the fly to follow more closely the movement of the notch and relying upon a smaller margin of escapement to prevent blocking? So many factors have to be considered, including the setting up of the hammer in the action-butt, the angle the hammer-head bears to the shank; the set-up of the action in the piano; the depth of touch, &c. It is seemingly impossible to give an answer. The very large variation in upright action design shows that a majority of its makers are far from being copyists, but are always endeavouring to obtain the ideal touch, blow, damping, escapement, and facility for repetition.

Fig. 48 (on page 98) shows the Model 10 Schwander action. This action has a splendid attack; it is fitted with jack, butt and damper-returning springs; also the jack spiral spring. The plate-centres to the butts facilitate adjustment. This Schwander No. 10 is made by Herrburger, Brooks of London. The firm of Brooks was founded in 1810, and its growth has followed the development of action-making as an industry apart from piano manufacture. With the exception of Erard's, Brooks's is the oldest action house in the world. The organisation of Herrburger (under the name of Schwander) was established in France about 1844. The fusion of the French and English houses was completed in 1920.

Erard's was established in Paris in 1780, and in London about 1792; and though not strictly an action-house, has given more to the advancement of piano-action construction than any other organisation. Erard's continue to manufacture their own actions, and, although in some ways conservative, the output is always of exceptional merit. In the field of the upright action, Erard's make to-day an *underdamper* action which operates on two strings for the soft pedal. Further, this is accomplished with a fixed keyboard; and there is no derangement causing "lost motion." That this pedal bestows definite tonal advantages is undoubted: so far as pedals are concerned, this Erard action converts an upright into a grand or horizontal instrument.

The question may well be asked, How is the lateral movement accomplished without interference with the dampers? (In an overdamper model the difficulty is small.) The explanation is that the rail which carries the dampers is not fixed to the beam: it has a separate fixing on the standards and is rigid. The beam and the hammers move over at will with a surprisingly easy movement to meet only two strings. The tail of the damper-arm is sufficiently wide to be operated from the jack-lever extension, whatever its position; and the width of the rear end of the key is easily sufficient to give a responsive attack to the prolonge, whether the left pedal is depressed or otherwise.

Fig. 74 shows the Canadian Higel design. This is an action of exceptional merit. It is interesting to notice the nomenclature employed by the makers (Messrs. Otto Higel, of Toronto), which can be seen in the explanation of the figure. Such words as catch-shank, wipp, abstract, tongue-flange, fillester-head-screw, hammer-rail shell, &c., seem strange to English action workers.

From the illustrations it will be seen that both the Schwander No. 10 and the Higel possess the facility for aligning the butts without removing the action from its position in the instrument.

(Note point 43 at rear of jack: Fig. 74.) The "spring rail spring" (point 23) is really a butt-returning spring, having the same effect as the spring in the Schwander No. 10: but in the Higel design the spring rail not only gives a fixing for the spring, but also acts as a damper slap rail.

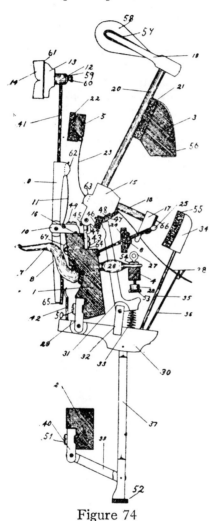

Figure 74

7 Damper rod
8 Damper rod nut
9 Damper lever
10 Damper lever flange
11 Damper lever spring
12 Damper block
13 Damper head
14 Damper felt
15 Butt
16 Brass butt flange
17 Catch
18 Catch shank
19 Hammer head
20 Hammer shank
21 Hammer rail cloth
22 Spring rail felt
23 Spring rail spring
24 Stop rail felt
25 Stop rail screw
26 Regulating rail prop
27 Regulating rail screw
28 Regulating rail button
29 Wipp flange
30 Wipp
31 Jack
32 Jack flange
33 Jack spring
34 Back check
35 Back check wire
36 Bridle wire
37 Abstract
38 Bridle strap
39 Tongue
40 Tongue flange
41 Lever wire
42 Spoon
43 Butt flange screw
44 Brass flange plate
45 Brass flange plate screw
46 Butt felt
47 Butt leather
48 Butt under cloth
49 Damper lever flange screw
50 Wipp flange screw
51 Tongue flange screw
52 Abstract cloth
53 Regulating rail punch
54 Fillister head screw for reg. rail
55 Back check felt
56 Hammer rail shell
57 Hammer under felt
58 Hammer felt
59 Damper block socket screw
61 Damper head under felt
62 Damper lever punching
63 Butt punching
65 Lever cloth
66 Catch leather
67 Damper rod nut screw

1 Action main rail
2 Bottom rail
3 Hammer rail
4 Regulating rail
5 Spring rail
6 Stop rail

CHAPTER IX

The Hammer

I T would be a mistake to imagine that the Cristofori action of itself made the piano. The small wood-block (see Fig. 50, page 102), covered with soft leather, which was equally a distinguishing feature of the mechanism, further separated the new instrument from all others. The action itself was a revolutionary device: it was the mechanism of percussion. The piano is the one instrument in which the strings are *struck*. It is not surprising, therefore, that in this instrument the material of percussion is of such importance.

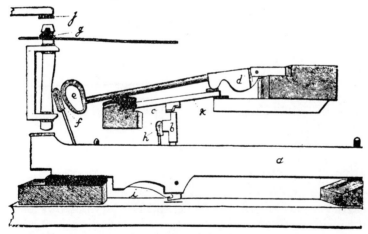

Figure 75

a = the key.

b the hopper (linguetta mobile = moveable tongue, Cristofori called it).

c the notch for the hopper beneath a lever lettered k. This lever, covered with leather upon the end, raises hammer-butt d.

e = the hammer head, covered with leather.

The spring i, under the key, maintains the position of the hopper in the notch, assisted by the small hopper check h.

The hammer check is f, the damper g. The damper stop is j.

129

Cristofori eventually introduced the tapered form of hammer (see *e* in Fig. 75, which shows the final stage of the Cristofori action).

Sheepskin, elkskin, German tinder, and very soft buckskin were also used for covering before the introduction of the felted hammer.

The process of "felting" is very old. The ruins of Pompeii have yielded a complete plant for scouring and pressing felts. The hairs of many animals are capable of being felted, because their hair, far from being smooth, is covered with imbrications; and when the fat present with the living animal is removed, these scale-like projections make a complete entanglement quite easy.

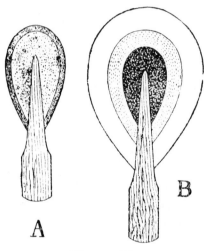

Figure 76

The Paris maker, Henri Pape, about 1839, exhibited pianos in which the hammers were covered with hair-felt. Fig. 76 (A) shows the early leather-covered hammer, and Fig. 76 (B) shows a hammer covered with leather and felt. Even in recent years rabbit fur has been used on the Continent; but it seems unlikely that a more suitable material than sheepswool felt will be discovered for covering the piano hammer.

A musically perfect string yields, when excited by an instantaneous blow from the hammer, the series of harmonics in definite relative intensity. But many influences are at work in the piano which prevent the ultimate tone from being as harmonic as the vibrations of the string might indicate. First, we listen not to the vibrations of a string itself. These would waste their sweetness on the desert air if it were not for the amplification of the impulses by the soundboard. With amplification comes a preferential treatment of some of the tonal components or partials. Other harmonics are weakened. The bridges, the belly and the casework of the piano modify the tone.

Again, the strings have a rigidity—a stiffness—of their own which plays a part in the quality of the tone given. Further, heavy blows undoubtedly increase the tension of the wire: whereas a light blow has little or no effect on the tension of the speaking length. A higher tension during vibration means a more complex tone.

A text-book theory is, of course, that to produce an ideal or mathematically perfect tone, the blow-point or striking-place must prevent any nodal conflict at the terminations of the speaking length. It follows, therefore, that the hammer should be quite hard and pointed at the nose. Practice softens these stipulations : instead of striking at a point, the surface of a bass hammer which meets the string is of a very appreciable length, and even the treble hammers have a definite length of striking face, as an examination of these hammers in any piano will prove.

The chief factor accounting for the difference between the theoretic tone the string should give and the tone ultimately produced is, however, the fact the hammer "follows through," and never gives an instantaneous contact. Moreover, the pressure-time curve of the felt in contact with the steel wire is not symmetrical. That is to say, the pressure exerted by the felt against the wire is less during the recoil period.[21] Slow motion photographic experiments have proved that the "follow through" of the hammer is a most important factor, for, if a hammer remains in adhesion with the steel wire more than the "periodic-time" of the string, the whole complexity of the string's movement is disorganised, and the hammer becomes a damper. The "periodic-time" of a string yielding 522 vs. per second is $\frac{1}{522}$ nd part of a second. A soft hammer will remain in contact for the

[21] The interesting point raised here is, Does a variation of touch, which means a variation of the speed of travel and consequently blow-power, affect the rebound of the hammer into check? Another influence at work which bears on this question, is the accuracy of the blow $qu\hat{a}$ blow. Any slew (such as happens when the sliding keyboard and action of the grand move during the contact of felt and steel), or any dither or wip of the hammer nose due to shank flexibility, affect adversely the purity of the tone.

whole of the periodic-time, but a resilient hammer of good quality will remain for only half the periodic-time.

The two essentials for a good covering material are, first that the material must be thoroughly felted. This ensures durability to combat the continual cutting by the steel wire. If the fibres are poorly connected, and also if the fibres are short, the wear is very rapid. The second essential is that the hammer must still possess extreme elasticity, to ensure a rapid recoil. The surface must be smooth and elastic, to produce a soft tone for *pianissimo* playing; yet there must be resistance sufficient to withstand the heavy blow of *fortissimo* playing.

The most serviceable and elastic wool comes from merino sheep raised in North America (Texas) or in the Cape, though it has been the custom to mix the wool from Australia, Africa and Eastern Europe (mostly Silesia), according to the result intended. The wool of the Australian merino sheep is peculiarly soft and fine (and thus less elastic), which makes it very well adapted for *damper* felt. American piano makers prefer to mix African and European wool with the American wool because it is believed that the American practice of bleaching destroys the elasticity, the fibres being broken. American makers to-day advertise the fact as a point of merit that they use imported hammer felt. The care given to rearing the sheep and the methods of cleaning and handling the wool, and the properties of the water used in the process, are reflected in the elasticity of the finished product.

One hundred pounds of raw wool, as it comes from the sheep's back, yields only twenty-five pounds of workable wool, seventy-five per cent. being lost in scouring. The next process is drying and opening, and the wool is then hardened and fulled until the mass coheres, without any trace of cement or chemicals, soap and hot water only being used. The required density is obtained by pressure.

Piano hammer making is to-day a distinct industry, both in Europe and America, the hammer maker purchasing the felt from the few firms who have specialised in the manufacture of the material from the wool. Whitehead Bros. of London (successors to the Wandle Felt Co.) are said to have been the first who made the manufacture of piano felt a specialty. Naish of Wilton started in 1859. Not only do piano makers obtain their actions from an independent auxiliary industry, but the piano hammer is almost invariably made by the piano hammer maker.

With the demand for a greater volume of tone, came heavier strings and a hammer capable of giving a more powerful blow.

The hand-made hammer was unsatisfactory, and various attempts were made to construct machines for gluing felt to the wooden moulding. Rudolf Kreter of New York, about 1850, patented a machine which covered the complete set in one operation: it was ingenious but complicated. It is recorded that this machine was eventually purchased as a curiosity by Brooks of London.

In 1887 Alfred Dolge patented a hammer covering machine built upon the principle of drawing the felt upward by the aid of an inclined plane on which the side cauls travel. During the past forty years there have been many improvements in hammer covering machines. The hand-made hammer was not used later than about 1880.

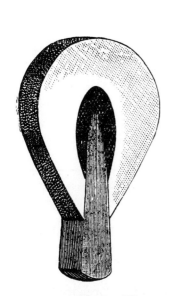

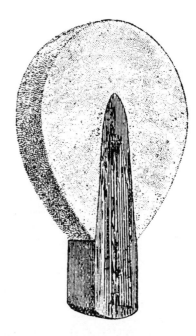

Figure 77   Figure 78

Fig. 77 shows a "double coated" English hammer. The "single coat" is regarded by some to be superior.

Fig. 78 shows a "single coated" hammer. It is thought that the extra cost of the single-coated hammer is justified by the evenness of the tone throughout the set. The double-covered hammer gives a better appearance, and it is claimed that the double-coat permits of a more gradual increase of firmness from the nose backwards to the wood moulding: though this is, we think, doubtful.

A sheet of felt suitable for covering a set of hammers by machine is anything from 8lb. to 18lb. in weight. The sheet is shrunk to about 2 cm. thick at the bass end, and 4 mm. or 5 mm. thick at the treble. It is about 90 cm. in length, the width of the striking face of a hammer being 1 cm. The gradation is not regular, it being good practice to belly the felt,—that is, to give a greater proportionate thickness to the notes from, say, C^{28} to C^{64}, where the wear is considerable.

The complete set is covered in one operation, the felt strip being made to the shape shown in Fig. 79 (B). The strip is bent up and glued around the hammer mouldings (Fig. 79, A), the hammers being cut apart when thoroughly dry.

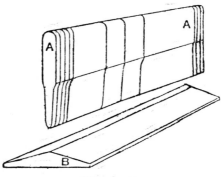

Figure 79

The hardness of a sheet is equal throughout, but the density of the felt in any finished hammer is greatest at the centre of the felt next to the wood moulding, and is less as the outer surface is approached.

Fig. 80 shows the bass end of a piece of felt as prepared to be glued around the moulding. To attain durability in the finished hammer, it is necessary that the trimmed side of the felt be glued up next to the wood, as illustrated in Fig. 80. If the flat side is placed next to the wood-head, the felt, under wear, loses its stratified formation and the layers crop out. It is the minute imbrications or serrations in the wool which facilitate "felting;" and, if the entanglement of these is destroyed, the hammer loses its resilience. The tension of the striking face is lost. Cutting the felt to a "roof" shape prevents the nose flattening.

A glance at Fig. 80 will show that the hot metal cauls of the covering machine must necessarily subject the felt to great compression at the moulding, but, at the outer skin, the felt is considerably stretched and is in great tension. This gradation from tension to compression is very important, for it determines the relative intensities of prime and partial tone components. It determines the quality of tone.

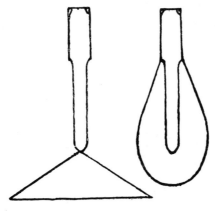

Figure 80

The production of the best quality of tone of which a given piano is capable is the work of the piano toner; and, although the standard is one subject to variations of taste, good toning is a matter of instinct and experience. Toning relaxes undue strain of the felt-covering of hammers. This relaxation should be done without affecting the elasticity of the striking face.

Toning is often necessary to remove an objectionable quality of tone at places where the bridge is cut away to allow passage of the iron-frame bars. (It is interesting to note that in some pianos, where the transmission of the impulses from the string to its support is slow and poor at the "break," the lack of resistance offered by the wire to the blow seems to be felt by the player at the ivory end of the piano key.)

Piano tuners, when sandpapering hammers, often imagine the white dust which comes away to be chalk. As a matter of fact, it is pure wool ground down by the sandpapering strip.

The ideal hammer is that which is capable of bringing all the tone out of the strings without arousing discordant partials which give an objectionable clang-tint. When piano tone is really good it does not change much in *quality* whether the playing be heavy or light.

If a single needle be pushed through a hammer at various points along a line drawn between the moulding and the outer surface (see Fig. 81, A), it will be found that the hardness decreases regularly as the outer face is reached. At the moulding, the felt is in compression : at the string-face it is in tension.

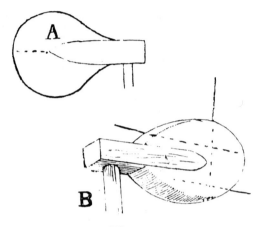

Figure 81

The density of the felt covering decreases as the outer surface is approached : thus, to relieve considerable compression the hammer should be pricked as indicated in Fig. 81 B.

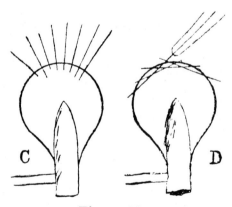

Figure 82

It is not often that the excess of hardness of hammers is such as to require the treatment indicated in Fig. 81 B, and a good quality of tone is usually to be obtained by shallow pricking in a radial direction, as shown in Fig. 82 C. Excessive tension of the striking-face should be eased by pricking the felt as shown in Fig. 82 D.

Steinway's some years ago adopted the expedient of cutting away a portion of the felt from the upper and under edges of the hammers, thereby relaxing undue strain without destroying the elasticity of the nose. These hammers had a most curious appearance.

Fig. 83 shows a suggested form of hammer head in which the felt is clasped within wooden prongs. This idea has lately been resuscitated in America.

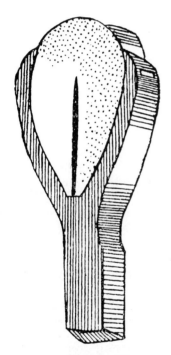

Figure 83

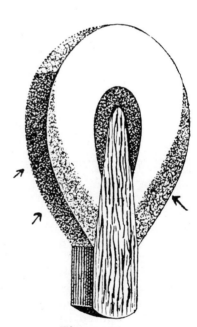

Figure 84

With the present method of covering hammers, it is difficult to obtain a sharp-pointed hammer, which means that the nose under heavy playing tends to flatten out; this is inimical to good tone. It was Steinway's who saturated with a hardening solution part of the felt (as shown in Fig. 84), to prevent the flattening of the head.

Fig. 85 illustrates a shape of hammer favoured by German makers.

Figure 85

Over-toning of hammers can only be remedied by a con-solidation of the felt with pressure from a hot iron. Undue softening of the felt by too much pricking results in the tone being very soft, the hammers clinging longer to the strings. It is a fact that hammers which are round-nosed across the face pro-duce a better tone than those which are slightly concave or quite flat. The hammers in Erard pianos are very often given a distinct rounding.

A thin covering of felt gives a soft tone: whereas the heavily covered hammer gives a full, ample tone. The hard, glittering, almost metallic quality of tone—which, providing it is free from clang, is admired by some pianists — is probably due among other things to a certain hardness in the texture of the felt rather than to excessive tension in the striking face.

To obtain brightness of tone in the extreme treble hammers, the felt is often touched with collodion or a little white French polish.

The angle which the hammer makes with the string when in

contact is of some importance, it being essential that the hammer gives a square clean blow. If the shank has a backward angle at the moment of contact, it follows that the hammer head must be inclined downwards some 2° or 3° if the blow is to be rectangular to the strings. Fig. 86 illustrates this point.

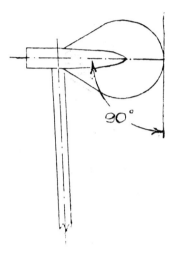

Figure 86

CHAPTER X

The Keyboard

HISTORICAL.

THE keyboard is a labour-saving device. That it is very old is indubitable. The *Cheng*, a Chinese instrument of great antiquity, is a crude form of organ in which a number of bamboo reed pipes stand in a bowl-shaped base. (See Fig. 87.) When a finger *covers* a hole in a bamboo pipe, wind being supplied from a mouthpiece, the pipe speaks: the finger is released, and the note ceases. Surely this is the embryonic stage of the modern clavier.

The form of *Hydraulus*, or hydraulic organ, which was in use about the first century of our era, possessed keys. These keys were "about eight inches long and two inches wide, naturals and inflected notes being all in one continuous row."[22] An eleventh century monk, Theophilus, has written of organs operated by perforated sliders (*linguæ*). But it seems more than likely that, during the period covered by his writings, there was also a balanced keyboard in use. The keys, no doubt, were very wide, because the idea of key-splaying, which paved the way for a compact keyboard, had not been developed. About the fourteenth century, organ keys were so wide that it took the whole weight of the hand to overcome their resistance. A key would be *pressed* down or struck with the side of a clenched fist. Notwithstanding these facts, records prove that the elevated semitone was in use at this period, and even earlier.

To some extent early paintings and miniatures supply illustrations of early *keyboard* forms. The information which these paintings give of actual musical instrument construction is not very helpful.

[22] "Keys and Stops," by Andrew Freeman (contained in No. 2 of *The Organ*, p. 75).

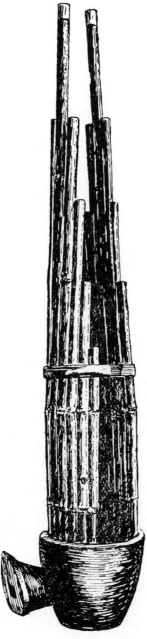

Figure 87

There is an authentic representation of a chromatic keyboard, painted not later than 1426, in the St. Cecilia panel of the famous Adoration of the Lamb by the Van Eycks. The instrument depicted is a portative (or positive) organ, and it is interesting to notice that the keys are apparently boxwood, and that the angel plays a common chord.

A picture by Fra Angelico (fifteenth century), in the National Gallery[23] (No. 663, in the Catalogue), shows a portative organ with accidentals.

The Italian monk, Guido d'Arezzo (995-1050), who is said to have invented the terms *Ut* (do), *Re*, *Mi*, *Fa*, *Sol*, *La*, is credited with having adapted a keyboard to polychord stringed instruments. But there are no reliable records as to who first applied the chromatic scale. Guido's diatonic scale was the basis of the diatonic keyboard. (See Fig. 88.)

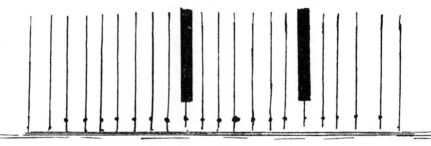

Figure 88

The diatonic organ keyboard with eight steps or keys in the octave, which included the B flat and the B natural, was long preserved, for Prætorius, an historian of the organ, speaks of it as existing later than 1600. This keyboard, we learn from Sebastian Virdung ("Musica Gesutscht und Auszgezongen": Basel, 1511), and Encyclopædia Britannica, 1911, Vol. 21, p. 560, was the keyboard of the early clavichord. The same writer attributes the introduction of the chromatic order to the endeavour to restore the three musical *genera* of the Greeks,—the diatonic, chromatic and enharmonic.

[23] This painting by Fra Angelico (1387-1455) is said to be a fine example of the heightened and convincing sense of motion of the Florentine School. The picture is in Room I. of the National Gallery. Another picture of interest is The Music Master (No. 856, Dutch School), by Jan Steen (1626-1679). The cheerful and homely humour of the painting is striking ; as also is the dexterity of colour and finish, for, although small, the alternating blocks of inflected notes are very clear.

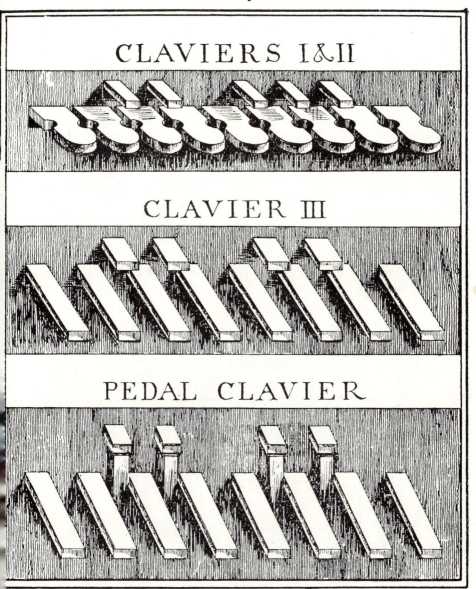

Figure 89

The earliest instance of the complete chromatic arrangement is that of the organ at Halberstadt, built in 1361 by Nicholas

Faber and restored in 1495 by Gregory Kleng. An inscription on the keyboard states that it formed part of the original organ, which had the semitonal arrangement of keys.

The Halberstadt instrument (1361) possessed an independent pedal department, and chromatic pedals were used extensively by early Continental organ builders.

Michael Prætorius (1571-1621)), an early historian of the organ, in his Syntagma Vol. 11 (1619), has preserved for us a representation of the four keyboards of the Halberstadt instrument, and a reproduction is shown on the previous page (Fig. 89),

The naturals of the two upper manuals were from three to four inches wide, and were obviously designed for "thumping." The third manual was designed for grasping rather than hitting. (One suggestion is that this manual was intended to be played with the knees, though it is difficult to understand how the sharps could be struck.) The fourth keyboard was played by the feet.

A French pedal-board (really a box) is illustrated in Fig. 90. It was made by Boizard, of Sedan, in 1714, for Saint-Michel-en-Thierache, and was in use as late as 1919, and perhaps later.

Figure 90

An organ erected in the Church of St. Blasius at Brunswick in the year 1499 (by one Heinrich Crantz) possessed keys of almost the same shape and dimensions as those now in use. (See Fig. 91.) The sharps of this instrument were coloured black.

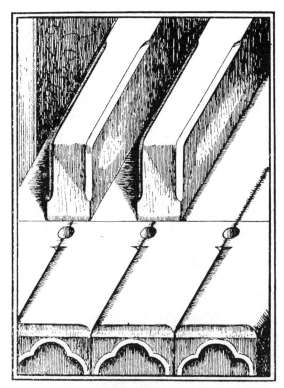

Figure 91

The colour of the keys has varied from time to time, but the ornamental effect of making the inflected notes a different colour to the naturals was soon introduced. A pertinent and authoritative quotation reads:—

"In England, during the sixteenth and seventeenth centuries, the custom was to make the naturals of ebony, and the sharps of ivory or bone. A richly ornamental appearance was often obtained by carving the front ends of the naturals, and by inlaying a strip of ebony or some rarer material along the length of each of the sharps. Samuel Green (d. September 14th, 1796) is said to have been the first to introduce the now universal custom of white naturals and black sharps. A fair number of the old 'black' keyboards still remain."

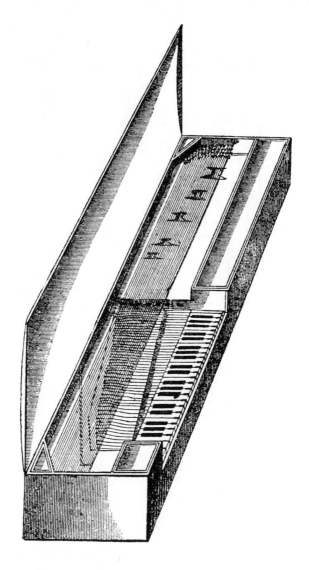

Figure 92

Fig. 92 shows a clavichord of the early sixteenth century with the modern chromatic scale.   In Fig. 93 we have the richly ornamented keyboard of an Italian spinet (*c.* 1577).

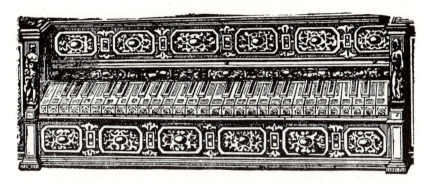

Figure 93

Fig. 94 shows a table clavier made by one Joh. Socher in 1742. The inscription thereon reads: "Joh. Socher im Obern Sonthofen, Allgäu, 1742." This *Hammerklavier* has a "black"

Figure 94

keyboard of four-and-a-half octaves. It is said only recently (1925) to have come to light, some notice of it having appeared in the German technical press.

Fig. 95 shows a Louis Quinze clavichord (1772), with a five-octave keyboard.

Figure 95

It is to be seen that the keyboard of the organ and of stringed instruments had influenced musical thought centuries before the invention of the piano. (It was about 1720 before Cristofori had fully developed his piano action. The figure given as a frontis-piece of this book is an illustration of one of Cristofori's pianos, dated 1726. The compass is four octaves. This instrument is now in the Kraus Museum, Florence. An earlier instrument, dated 1720, is in the Metropolitan Museum, New York.)

We have said that the keyboard was a labour-saving device. This is true in the sense that it enabled the musician to indicate, if not to sustain, a much larger number of notes than was pos-sible on the lute or similar instrument. Further, the develop-ment of the clavichord, harpsichord, &c., with the slight resist-ance of their mechanism, permitted complicated and rapid successions of notes. The early organ permitted only a meagre accompaniment, the notes being sustained with the aid of collaborators at the bellows.

Coming down to more recent times, it must be observed that the influence of the keyboard on the development of music is as conspicuous as it is important. Our present keyboard, with its alternating blocks of two and three inflected notes (Fig. 96), giving twelve notes to the octave, has stood the test of something like six hundred years. The fingers of Palestrina, Zarlino, Byrd, John Bull and J. Sebastian Bach — and those of Mary and Elizabeth Stuart — have conformed to the same keyboard as have the hands of Clementi, Beethoven, Chopin, Liszt, and Ignaz Paderewski. It is apposite to recall what Huxley says :—

" The ingenuity of human inventions has been paralleled by the tenacity with which original forms have been preserved."

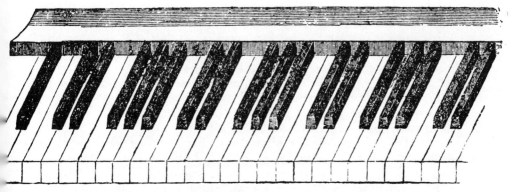

Figure 96

Fig. 96 shows the isolated inflected note (A$\sharp^2$), and the recurring blocks of two and then three inflected semitones of the modern clavier.

One may wonder if the present clavier has been worthy of such preservation. It has had, of course, a controlling influence over musical temperament. But the fascinating question which leaps to the mind is, *Why* such an irregular and illogical form ? Has this arrangement been due solely to the desire to adapt the keys to the diatonic scaling, coupled with the facility to employ any key as a new root or tonic ? Musical antiquaries are unable to explain adequately the reason for the *form* of the range. Hipkins expressed his conviction that early organ keyboards (and so the keys of the spinet, &c.) followed the Greek system of music:

the compass of early keyboards coinciding with a Greek tetra-chordal scale.

When it is remembered that the diatonic scale intervals are:

$$
\begin{array}{lll}
\text{C to D} & : & \text{1 whole tone} \\
\text{D to E} & : & \text{1 whole tone} \\
\text{E to F} & : & \text{1 semitone} \\
\text{F to G} & : & \text{1 whole tone} \\
\text{G to A} & : & \text{1 whole tone} \\
\text{A to B} & : & \text{1 whole tone} \\
\text{B to C} & : & \text{1 semitone,}
\end{array}
$$

a moment's thought will show that, if the tonic note of a progression is elevated by one semitone, it is possible to complete the diatonic scale within the thirteen keys of the keyboard octave. If C♯ is taken for the keynote of a scale, the next full tone is to D♯, the next to F♮. An additional key between E and F is unnecessary, the relationship of E♮ to F♮ being that of a semitone.[24] The outstanding feature of the keyboard of to-day is that it permits of complete modulation. The full range of the octave is thirteen notes: this, of course, providing twenty-four modes.

The invention of the raised note has been associated with Gioseffo Zarlino, a musical theorist of Venice (1517-1590); but, as we have shown, the chromatic scale as embodied in the keyboard existed as far back as 1361 (Halberstadt).

A Dr. Krause, of Eisenberg, was one who rebelled against inflected semitones, and he constructed in 1811 a keyboard in which all the notes were of one colour and were at one level.

Although the system of equal temperament was understood some time prior to the period when J. S. Bach (1685-1750) wrote his Forty-eight Preludes and Fugues, we can say that it was not until about 1850 that it was adopted universally. To-day, when Sir Richard R. Terry condemns the piano because it destroys a sense of just intonation, he is really condemning the *keyboard* of the piano. There is no difficulty in providing more *strings* to

[24] It is interesting to observe that our "common" key commences with the letter C, and runs C, D, E, F, G, A, B, C. The sequence which follows the letters A, B, C, D, E, F, G, A (and requires a G♯ instead of G) is an ancient Greek diatonic scale which lasted through the break-up of ancient civilisation, and was used by the early monks. When letters were first used to distinguish musical tones, the monks named this system of seven (the sacred seven notes of music) with the first seven letters. Later, when the power and possibilities of the major scale were realised, the third note (C) of the ancient Greek scale was taken as the principal keynote and starting point for music.

the octave. Pure intonation on a keyed instrument is a commercial, and almost a mechanical, impossibility. The quarter-tones found on the old organ at the Temple Church (see Fig. 97), at Durham Cathedral and elsewhere, recall the use of unequal or mean-tone divisions of the octave.

Figure 97

The Greeks knew well enough that the central problem of intonation is insoluble: that the tiny interval, known as the Pythagorean comma, cannot be eliminated. Scientific and practical musicians, mathematicians, and others, have ever been trying to conceal its existence, and to obtain the advantage of having all keys perfectly in tune. General Perronet-Thompson's organ, with forty pipes to the octave; the Bosanquet keyboard; and the unique keyboard designed by the Japanese scientist, Dr. Shohé Tanaka. These are all attempts to bring more material to the service of the musician without loss of the facility for modulation. Dr. Shohé Tanaka's suggestion was to have an octave of twenty steps by means of a system of divided keys. It is claimed that the system is very easy to grasp.

To-day the piano plays such an important and dominating part in the lives of musicians that few realise that its fifths are flat and that its major thirds are abominably sharp. The average ear readily accepts the incisive "salt-like" quality of a sustained major third or sixth on the organ. The ineffable beauty of a pure chord is, to the great majority, a thing unknown. Though it is true that there are some who regard absolute consonance as a saccharine ingredient of milk-music.

Many pregnant questions can be asked concerning the keyboard of the future. Will the Clutsam concave-board (as illustrated in Fig. 98) find favour? Has the Jankó-Perzina (1910) arrangement a place to fill? Are the manuals and couplers of Emanuel Moor, to which Dr. Donald Tovey has given such unqualified blessing, merely the outcome of a restless, inventive, but impractical mind?

Figure 98

The idea of restricting the sweep of the pianist's arm to a semicircle is not new, for a piano maker (Neuhaus) of Vienna is said to have built a concave board about 1780.

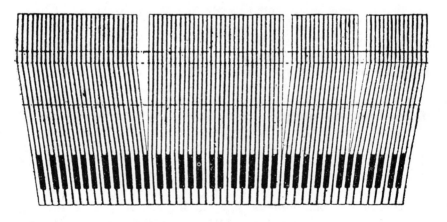

Figure 99

An interesting suggestion, which was patented a few years ago, was to include the ivory-covered lengths of the keys in the splaying, which meant that the keys radiated from an imaginary centre *behind* the player's back.   (See Fig. 99.)

The question of how far the masterpieces of musical art would suffer distortion by adaptation to those temperaments which provide just intonation for selected keys cannot be discussed here. Perhaps the breadth and majesty of a master's conception is proof against the more minute alterations in the pitch relationship of the scale tones.

The outstanding fact is that it is the present form of keyboard which has given the greatest facility to the development of musical art.   (The gramophone, the player piano, wireless reception, &c., are, of course, merely new disseminators of a form of music which is dictated by the equal tempering of the keyboard tones.)

THE MODERN KEYBOARD.

The modern clavier is possibly six hundred years old : but for those who have the seeing eye, its eighty-eight notes represent over two thousand years of musical romance and development !

Fig. 100 shows an individual natural key.

The piano key is a lever of the first order which does its work beyond the fulcrum (note Fig. 100), in which it is in contrast to the harmonium key.

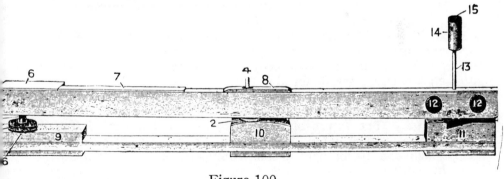

Figure 100

1 Front washer	7 Tail	13 Pilot (or dolly) wire
2 Balance washer	8 Chase	14 Pilot (or dolly) top
3 Front pin	9 Front rail	15 Pilot (or dolly) pad
4 Balance pin	10 Balance rail	16 Paper washer
5 Front	11 Back rail	17 Back touch
6 Head	12 Key lead	

In the early days of piano making, linden was used almost exclusively for keys, the logs being cleft. For many years, owing to the scarcity of the lime tree, Swiss pine or American bass has taken its place. The board should never less than 1 in.; and, if the keys are long, as in grands and players, $1\frac{1}{16}$ in. is preferable.

Key mortices, in good class work, are always bushed. It is essential that all cloth shall be soft, to make for silence, yet firm to avoid loss of power. Cheap instruments of German make often have no front baizes: or sometimes one strip of cloth is glued along the length of the front key rail, the key movement being limited at the far end with a back-touch rail. This gives a springy feeling and is objectionable. In spite of various methods of strengthening the front rail of the key-frame, a movement sometimes occurs, and in these cases a back-touch rail would prevent blocking. A combination of front and back touches is perhaps the best arrangement. A very thin boxcloth for the balance rail is often used; this may be good where dampness would attack a thick washer, but as soon as the key is worn at the balance hole, noise develops.

The oval front pin is often misused. The bat shape is adopted to give a wide face to the cloth bushing. Careless easing of the mortices when the keys are laid can, however, be remedied by increasing the effective diameter of the pin; so also, of course, can compensation be given for wear. But, when an instrument passes out from the regulator, the major axis of the pin should be quite parallel to the clef line of the keys.

Fig. 101 shows the lay-out of the twelve keys of the modern keyboard. The piano key is a simple lever which conveys without any avoidable loss the force put forth by the fingers of the performer, and as such conforms to the elementary laws of mechanics. It is doubtful if the individual key, considered as a transmitter of power, can be improved: but the arrangement of the keys coming within the stretch of the hand is a very different matter. The future of the piano, and perhaps the future of musical temperament, is subservient to the set-out of the keys which can be brought within command of the stretch of the human hand.

The illustration (Fig. 101) shows the complete septave, which is the unit of the $7\frac{1}{3}$ octave keyboard. The key in this example is 16in.; the operative length $14\frac{1}{8}$in.; the front balance 8in.; the splaying, which enables the front standard scale to meet the pilot or strike scale, commencing at 6in. from the front, to which point the covering of the naturals extends; the distance from the

Treble String

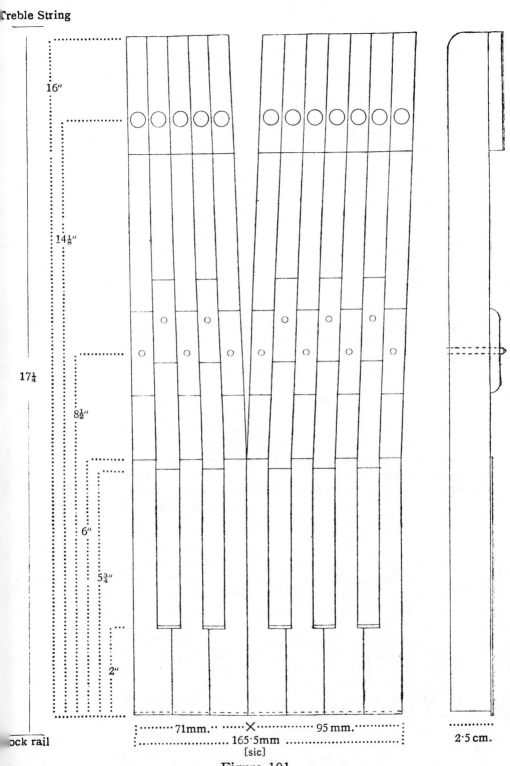

16″

14⅛″

17¼

8½″

6″

5¾″

2″

ock rail

71mm.   ✕   95 mm.

165·5mm
[sic]

2·5 cm.

Figure 101

front of the natural key to the rear of the sharp is 5¾in.; this gives approximately ¼in. of nameboard cloth; the length of the key-head is 2in.

A writer on musical subjects (Dr. Percy Buck) has suggested that one of the explanations of the phenomenon of key-colour is that the raised keys of the keyboard give a reduced lift to their action sections, and therefore the touch and blow: and so the ultimate tone varies when a composition passes into a key which chiefly employs the raised keys. It may be true that the facility for rapid execution is increased when the black keys constitute the basis of a composition; but the raised key has the same touch-depth and the same weight of touch as the natural. A glance at Fig. 101 shows the front and back balances of the white keys are 8½in. and 5⅝in. (total 14⅛in.). Now, the figures for the raised keys are 7⅕in. and 4⅘in. (total 12in. *circa*). Both these sets of figures agree to the ratio of 3 : 2. To achieve this, the balance rail carries two rows of pins. Action makers state what key balances are necessary to give the hammer a path of 5 cm., with a touch depth of 10 mm., these measurements being accepted as standard. Where there is considerable height between the key and the action jack-lever, a small increase in the lift-balance must be given to compensate for loss due to circular motion. Action lever centres are positioned to give a horizontal line to the lever when the key is half depressed. And it is customary for the natural keys to be so laid that when half depressed, they too are horizontal; when at rest, therefore, these keys have a slight angle, corresponding to 5 mm. in about eight or nine inches. When looking at a keyboard, this small angle seems greater than it is, due to the fact that the sharps are much higher at their fronts; the surfaces are sometimes very considerable slanted off.

The key should be regarded as an extension of the action: the two units must work together with the minimum of friction. The degree to which the foot or block of the jack lever comes forward, so must the pilot follow. It may be asked, which is to be accepted as the standard in determining the sweep of the pilot head, the 52 white keys or the 36 raised keys. In drawing the arc which will show the path of the attacking pilot, a point is selected midway between the underside or rocking point of the naturals and the sharps; this ensures that the natural key gives practically the same degree of lift to its hammer section as does the sharp.

The standard measurements for the septave of the modern keyboard is 165'5 mm. (See Fig. 101.) The total length of the keyboard is arrived at as follows: 165ʻ5 × 7 = 1158ʻ5 mm., this figure being the length of the seven octaves, C^4 to B^{87}, that is, the distance from the first to the last clef. (The word "clef" probably came into use because the key-maker's saw travels right through the board at the division between B and C, and also between E and F, the board being completely cleft at these points.) To 1158ʻ5 mm. must be added the width of the two notes at the bass, A^1 and B^3; and C^{88} at the treble, thus :—

Length of 7 octaves ... ... 115ʻ85 cm.
3 natural keys ... ... 7ʻ09 cm. (*c.*)

Total length of front key scale ... ... 122ʻ94 cm. (*c.*)
    (or 48 inches, approximately.)

The unit of the keyboard, the septave of 165ʻ5 mm. divides up as follows :—

    3 heads for the C, D, and E = 71 mm. = 23ʻ7 mm. each
    4 heads for the F, G, A, and B = 95 mm. = 23ʻ61 mm. each

Nine-tenths of an inch is therefore about the width of the natural key across the head. This makes the octave a convenient width. (Kirkman of London, in 1851, built a piano keyboard of 6¾ octaves, 2ft. 2½in. in length, this allowing only ½in. for each natural key.)

A recent examination of some new pianos of English, French, German and American manufacture has shown that the standard in all these countries conforms very closely to the figures given in Fig. 101. But, while this front key-scale is general, the divisions for the tails and sharps vary considerably, and it seems that only in high-grade keys are proper divisions of the clefs made.

If the 71 mm. of the C, D, E group are divided into 5 exactly equal divisions, the space for each note (tail or sharp) is 14ʻ2 mm. The F, G, A, B (95 mm.) group has to give 7 keys, and these, if set out equally, are of 13ʻ5 mm. Fig. 102 shows the latter group.

Should the sharps be overwide at the bottom (and often they as wide as 12 mm.), it becomes practically impossible for a player with short stubby fingers to play on the tails of G and A. The sharp should be not more than 10ʻ8 mm. at the base, tapering to 9ʻ8 at the top. In low-grade keys, errors in marking or cutting often result in the tails of G and A being only 11 mm. or 12 mm.

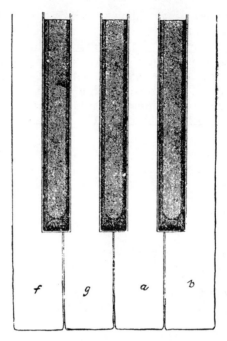

Figure 102

wide.   An average width for a middle finger of the male hand is
about 21 mm.   Even with the best setting-out, material, and
craftsmanship, the tails of the D, G, and A are dangerously
narrow, and this fact alone should force key-makers to buff the
edges of the heads: yet it is seldom done.   Another little
refinement seldom found is a slight rounding of the lip of the
heads.

An average width for the strike scale — and therefore the
hammer and pilot scale — for a $7\frac{1}{3}$ octave piano is, say, 125 cm.,
this including the breaks.   The front key-scale has been shown
to be 122'94 cm.: therefore the splay required by the piano key
is very small.   It need not, with skilful setting out by the scale
and frame designer, exceed half-an-inch.   Makers will sometimes
give a wide key splay merely to equalise the size of the treble
and bass key-blocks.   A very small point in appearance is gained
at the expense of the additional wear at the balance hole; and
the slight rolling motion is likely to affect the touch if the pilot is
too far out of the direct line of the key-head.

Touch.

Fig. 103 shows a set of keys for a grand piano. While the front key-scale is about the same total width as the action-scale, a double splay is used to adjust the one to the other. If properly regulated, the keyboard of the piano should have the appearance of being one solid block: the fronts of the keys should be perfectly square, and the keys themselves should be abso-

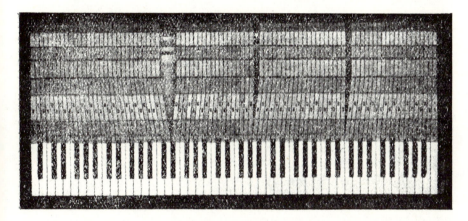

Figure 103

lutely level. The depth to which each key can be depressed must be exactly identical. These conditions are the prerequisites of a good touch, and by touch is meant the sensitive feeling imparted to the finger by the collective movement of key and action.

While differences in touch vary the speed of the descent of the key, no matter how the key is released, the speed of its ascent cannot be altered: it returns to rest in one fixed way as soon as the finger leaves it.

Differences in touch, so far as they affect the vibration of the string and so the ultimate tone, always involve differences in speed of key-descent. The key is merely a mechanism capable of being moved at its extremities through a (practically) vertical arc of about three-eighths of an inch, and this key is immovable in any other way. Musicians speak of a low-wrist touch; a non-percussive touch; a clawing touch; a high-wrist touch; a surface touch. Further, musicians distinguish certain tone-complexes by these distinctive terms: harsh, shallow, brilliant, mellow, round, forced, dry, steely, ringing, jarring, strident, clear, brittle, metallic, bell-like, velvety, and so forth.

It will be noticed that some of these terms are merely descriptive of tone-intensity: and, whatever term is applied to the manner in which a key is depressed, it can only describe the key-speed. That is, of course, the speed of descent through its path of three-eighths of an inch. The question of the time the key is kept down and the consequent control of the damping opens up other and entirely different problems. Key ascent may be retarded to any extent desired by the player, but cannot be advanced or increased in speed (except perhaps for a very slight increase resulting from pressure upon the key-pad which would be due to the elasticity of the felt.)

The weight of touch now in general use is 3 ounces in the lowest bass portion, graduated to about 2 ounces in the treble. This means that a 2 oz. or 3 oz. weight will just carry the hammer to the string. Back-loading of the key is required for upright pianos: at least at the treble end. Sometimes a loaded pilot is used. In grands, because of the weight of the action and hammers, it becomes necessary to load the front of the keys. The upward jump of the grand key cannot always be countered. Springs are sometimes used to carry part of the weight of the action unit and to avoid the front-key loading, though this is only done in the bass section.

Double touch, a device by means of which an organ key will speak at two strengths— softly if only partially depressed, and more loudly if pressed completely down—is a very old invention; and there have been efforts (all unsuccessful) to apply the idea to the piano. Double touch is of no practical utility even for the organ, though Erard in 1830 took out a patent for his "expressive touch."

KEY COVERING.

For the covering of the natural keys, ivory is, beyond doubt, the superior material. Its "feel" is excellent and it takes a beautiful polish; but it is expensive, changes colour, and a joint has to be made between the "head" and the "tail" of the key. (The standard of machine-work is such that this joint is practically invisible.) In the matter of substitutes, celluloid and "galalith" hold the field. Celluloid, a compound of nitrocellulose, camphor, &c., is less inflammable as now prepared, and wears well. Celluloid can be shaped round the key—head, tail and front—which is invaluable for keyboards built into pianos for the tropics. The covering can then be pinned at the lower edge of the front and at the back of the tail, and the pinning is practically invisible.[25] Galalith (literally, milkstone) comes from the casein of milk. In France, it is known as "elfinite:" it is a little liable to hygrometric changes, which cause it to shrink and crack.

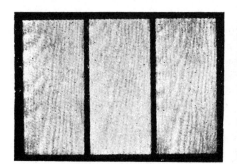

Figure 104

Figure 105

It is probable that supplies of ivory will not hold out long against the large demand. Some information about obtaining ivory may not be uninteresting. The African elephant is almost

[25] As an example of how efficacious in preventing separation due to moisture this pinning may be, the writer may mention that he has some keys taken from a piano which was on board a vessel sunk during the war. Later the vessel was raised. The celluloid covering is as firm as when the keys were made.

the exclusive source of ivory used for piano keys. The largest tusk ever obtained was over ten feet from base to tip along the outside curve, and the weight was over 230lb. The circumference at the hollow end was nearly 24in. The elephant is probably the shrewdest and most adaptable of animals and has no enemies except man. The beast can be diabolically ferocious, and will trample and roll upon its victims, man or animal, to be sure that its work of destruction is complete.

When an elephant is killed, the tusks are usually cut and chopped out of its head with knives and axes. The tusks must then be transported to the nearest rail-head or port, and the distance is often hundreds of miles.

Raw ivory costs about $5'00 a pound in New York, which market, with Amsterdam, controls the ivory supply of the world. A small tusk may weigh only 20lb. (The writer has seen at Messrs. Shenstone's Leyton works some tusks only a few inches in length, which it is believed the elephant sheds). The average tusk may be about 60lb., which could yield some thirty-seven sets of piano key coverings.

The thickness of ivory now used on keys is much less than in former times. This fact and the various systems of bleaching and matching the material helps to eke out the reducing quantity brought to Europe. Unfortunately, there is a prejudice against the figured ivory key. The highly figured ivory is preferred by makers of fine toilet articles, &c. It is curious that the piano maker should demand a high figure upon veneers, but insist that a rich figure is detrimental to the appearance of the piano key. Fig. 104 shows some beautiful examples of figured ivory key-heads, and Fig. 105 shows a key-covering of both figured and plain ivory. The key makers themselves have perhaps unconsciously fostered this prejudice against the figured ivory. There is more figured ivory in a tusk than plain.

CHAPTER XI

The Soundboard

SOUND is what is known as an effect caused by undulations of the air upon the drums of the ear. Exquisitely adapted transmitters make this effect known to the brain. The impulses, arriving at the ear, are best looked upon as differences of pressure on the ear-drum, which is pushed in and out thereby. Sound waves, which can be compared to the shells of an onion, are series of pushes and retreats of air particles; they are series of condensations and rarefactions, or "closing-ups" and "widenings-outs."

If a string of a piano could be isolated from the soundboard and agitated, very little sound would be heard: the reason being that the air would flow and reflow around the string, and the energy would be quickly exhausted. The strings of a piano are harnessed to the soundboard, instead of being allowed to waste their energy in a futile attempt to produce audible sounds unassisted: they are made to energise a large surface of board, which in turn moves large zones of air. A commensurate increase in the loudness of the sound is thus ensured; but there is no increase of energy. The impulses of the moving wire are more effectively employed. There is amplification with a corresponding loss of continuance. The strings of the violin are agitated during the whole time the notes are required to be audible. The problem for the violin maker is not complicated with the necessity for continuance. The piano has the great failing—or limitation—that, once produced, the tone cannot be varied, except by use of the pedals: further, the tone is fleeting.

If the sound as represented by the vibrating string of the piano is all that can be desired, then it is the duty of the soundboard to reinforce these vibrations *without change* of character and convey them to the air.

If, on the other hand, the vibrations of the string are defect-

163

ive—or imperfect—then it can be held that the soundboard has also to perform the duty of *improving* as well as reinforcing the original vibrations, so that the desired tone-quality is given by the instrument as a whole.   Unfortunately, the exact types of complex vibrations which are most acceptable as forming the ideal musical tone are matters of opinion and controversy.   And the exact dimensions of mechanical details of string, hammer, touch, bridge and soundboard required to produce these movements have never been tabulated.

One most important factor is the nature of the wood used for the board, for, be it noted, the wood structure can be made to respond to an infinite number of vibrations from the notes struck by the performer.   Not only does the structure respond to all the tonal components of the notes actually struck, but, with the sustaining pedal depressed, an incalculable number of vibrations are awakened by resonance.

That there is molecular friction within the wood is undoubted, but, to be effective, it must be translated to surface movements.

The soundboard may well be called the nervous system of the piano.   (The principles underlying the bellying and barring of pianos were understood, long before the piano was invented, by the early spinet and lute makers.)   The motion of the strings is communicated to the bridge by pressing the bridge in a direction parallel to the direction in which the strings are set vibrating by the hammer.   As a string returns from its position of maximum displacement, it swings almost as far in the opposite direction, and (*in the upright instrument*) tends to leave the bridge.   What prevents it from so doing?

> (*a*) The rake given to the wire by passing it round a bridge pin and then by a second pin forcing it back to its original direction.
>
> (*b*) The overhang of the bridge pin.
>
> (*c*) The momentary release of the down-pressure on the bridge, which allows the soundboard to recover its original position.

It is doubtful if the belly is "sucked up" at all, at any rate in the upright piano: rather is there a return to the normal position, for in the position of rest there is a downward pressure on the bridge, board and bars, which these latter resist with an equal force, action and reaction being equal but opposite.

It is here that we may find the reason for the curvature of the soundboard. If no curvature had been given, the down-bearing would have produced a tension which would be taken by the fillets, and any further movement of the bridge in the same direction would involve an extension of the bars in their length. The resistance of the bars would be very great. Piano makers always allow for the distortion of the belly, which follows when the "back" is chipped up to pitch. The condition aimed at is, that when the full downbearing is acting on the bridges (possibly amounting to half-a-ton), the soundboard shall retain its curvature and elasticity, and be in effect a mass of nerves responsive to the most minute shocks. If it is in the nature of a partly closed spring, it does not oppose the impressed vibrations of the wires. The hammer gives a momentary dent to the wire, and this dent travels along as a pulse to the points of support. Here it is reversed and travels back again.

MATERIAL.

Certain metals can be employed for piano soundboards, and the tone result is quite satisfactory. A metal soundboard is exceedingly responsive, due to its high rate of sound propagation: but the use of metal for soundboards is not within the scope of practical piano making. The great comparative weight, the extreme difficulties of making, fixing and adjusting, make it very unlikely that iron or aluminium will ever replace the board of coniferous wood.

The Norway spruce[26] is the wood primarily used by European makers for belly-wood. This wood is remarkably free from knots and is straight of grain; it is flexible and elastic, easy to work and transmits vibrations lengthwise of its grain at a very great rapidity,—over 15,000 ft. per second. This last fact is significant, for, while the soundboard is not used as a transmitter, it is likely to be more effective as a resonator if the impulses of the strings are rapidly distributed over its whole area. The bars of a soundboard are conveyors and distributors of energy as well as supports. The rate of travel of sound across the grain of firwood is only about 4000 ft. per second: a moment's consideration will show that the bars act as conveyors along their grain, thus causing a more rapid soundboard action.

[26] This is *Picea excelsa*, although it is commonly known as Swiss pine. Another wood used for bellying is the silver fir, or *Abies pectinata;* the *Picea alba* of the Western Hemisphere is used by American makers and has been imported freely into this country from Seattle and other timber ports.

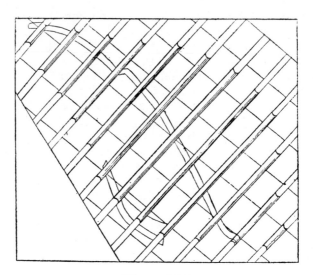

Figure 106

Fig. 106 shows a plan for a soundboard which is taken from Hansing. It is the general practice to place the grain of the bellywood parallel to a line drawn through the long bridge, the bars then running at right angles to the bridge. The low rate of travel of sound across the grain is thus countered by the action of the bars.

The thickness of the board when finished varies with the caprice of the maker, and it may be anything from 7 mm. to 10 mm. The practice of grading the thickness seems to be discarded. Some prefer to leave the board thicker at the treble, but nothing seems to be lost by finishing the board at an even thickness.

The ideal position for the bridge is, of course, that it should stand in the centre of the length of each bar: but this is impossible. It has been found advantageous to limit the size of the soundboard, because, if too large, it does not vibrate as a whole: some parts are in a different phase to the rest. This is the explanation of the cutting away of triangular pieces in the bottom treble and top bass corners, or of the use of *dumb bars* to make these portions of the soundboard ineffective. In the grand piano the shape itself limits the soundboard area at the treble end.

Figure 107

The figure shows the back of an upright piano which contains a grand form of rim ; this rim is about 14ft. in length, and 5in. in width. The illustration represents a form of construction which aims at capturing the "grand" tone for the upright instrument. No upright back is required, and the exact string lengths and the other lay-out which would belong to the horizontal grand proper are reproduced in the upright. In this upright-grand, the hammers, of course, still have to strike the strings from above, and so towards the soundboard surface.

The bars of the soundboard—usually about ten in number—are 2 cm. to 3 cm. square and are scalloped at the ends. The edges of the belly should be as rigidly fixed as is possible; indeed, a very rigid constraint is essential, so that the pulsations which travel from the bridges outwards are not allowed to escape, but will recoil with as little "leakage" as possible.

In the horizontal instrument, the pulsations are opposed by dense bands of hard wood, which constitute the bent inner rim, and of course a further outer rim is attached thereto. A hard-wood belly-rail continues where the rim is interrupted.

Such an excellent surround cannot easily be provided in the upright piano, although Fig. 107 (page 167) illustrates a bent rim for an upright instrument made by an American maker.

Figure 108

Fig. 108 shows a new form of upright back made by Broadwood's, in which a very solid surround is given to the soundboard.

The distribution of bars is often a subject of controversy, but certain rules seem to be established by custom. For example, it is held to be essential that at the point of the lowest note on the long bridge, a bar should intersect; the same condition to be observed at both ends of the bass bridge. Another rule is that the highest bar shall be beneath the fourth or fifth note. One essential is that bars shall not be wide and thin, for it must always be remembered that bars are supports or girders, and their strength therefore, varies directly as the width, and as the *square* of the depth.

The bridge is the link between strings and soundboard. Since the introduction of the iron frame, bridges have been much higher than was usual before the necessary clearance had to be allowed between the belly and the frame. The long bridge is $1\frac{1}{8}$ in. to $1\frac{1}{2}$ in. in height; the bass-bridge being higher than this by the degree to which the bass strings are elevated above the steels,—about 1in. in 4ft. (It is worth while considering for a moment the great comparative height of the violin bridge.) No definite ratio between string tension and height of bridges has ever been formulated. Some say that an improvement in quality and in power and continuance follows an increase in height; certainly very good results are found in a long grand, where the bass bridge is very high. All the motions of the string are felt at the bridge, as minute shortenings and elongations, and the more responsive the bridge, the more free and round is the tone.

While necessity dictates the use of quartered beech, at least for the capping of the bridge, there is no reason why a wood that is lighter and less inelastic should not be employed to form the body: and spruce is frequently so employed. The most responsive bridge is made of $\frac{3}{16}$ in. or $\frac{1}{4}$ in. layers of maple or similar wood bent up, the joints being at right angles to the face of the soundboard.

This arrangement gives a continuity of grain; the bridge pins being driven right through the capping to the laminated portion. There are, of course, the disadvantages of excessive glue and the liability to opening in damp atmospheres; further, the cost is considerable. Alternate layers of Swiss pine and maple, bent up as described, will result in a very rapid transmission of the impulses of the string.

The cutting away of the depth of the bridge to clear the frame bars should be as shallow as possible, and made up for at the back of the soundboard.

The expedient of floating or suspending the bass bridge, which permits of a longer length of string and still allows the impulses to reach the board at a good distance from its dead and irresponsive ends, is very old: and the value of this system of bridging is beyond question. The best result is obtained when the slip or rail which joins the suspended portion to the board is carried far enough in each direction to lie over one or more bars beyond the width of the bridge itself. In the Blüthner aliquot-scaled pianos, a very beautiful example of suspended bridging can be seen where the small extra bridge for the unstruck wire is floated to carry the contact nearer to the main bridge and away from the inflexible edge of the soundboard.

To produce a tone which is as pure as the motions of the strings allow, it is essential that the notches on the bridges should be cut with accuracy to at least the middle of the bridge pin hole. The cut should be steep to permit of a good clearance between steel and wood. Expensive pianos have the steps carved hollow, and there are machines in some factories which do this work. One or two German makers cut a short vertical step, and then continue with a bevel to the edges of the bridges. This is difficult and requires a high standard of craftsmanship and supervision, but it does provide a distinct determination to the active length of the wire.

Where a bridge is capped, the carving should never be allowed to pare into the joint; it looks bad and allows the damp to attack the glue and weaken the adhesion.

The mill-made bridge is not a custom that has been adopted very widely in England, although the mill-made belly is very common for the reason that it removes an item of manufacture which occupies considerable space and requires skilled and tractable workmen. The disadvantages of the mill-made belly are that the thicknessing is not always accurate. A depression in the surface is due to the grain having been torn out by the planing machine, and after the use of the smoothing tools it is not readily visible. These slight depressions make it difficult to obtain good joints for the bars and bridges. Mill-made bellies are often made of narrow pieces, and this means numerous joints, and, if the matching is not good, a very patchy appearance.

The adjustment of the bearings with stock bridges is done by varying the iron-frame level and by using cushions thereon. A celebrated French house recently patented (British patent 193,806 / 1923 : Gaveau et Cie., Paris) what, in effect, was a process of piano manufacture. Fig. 109 is reproduced from this patent. It illustrates very well a method of mounting the belly on the back, and then the frame on the existing structure, bearing or sprace-blocks giving the required bearings for the strings.

An examination of Fig. 109 shows that the back, belly and frame are each capable of being adjusted in their distance from each other.

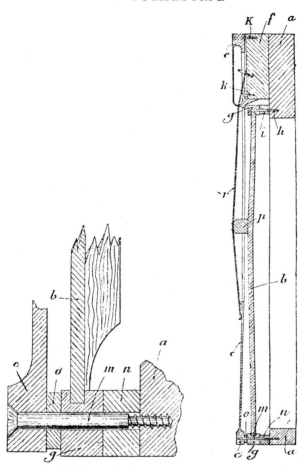

Figure 109

The back a, the soundboard b, and the frame c, form three removable elements. The soundboard b may be inserted and glued along its edges in an independent mounting frame g. For carrying out the mounting operation, one places the soundboard, provided with the mounting frame g, upon the framework a, disposed horizontally, space blocks i being interposed. The metal frame c, provided with holes k and m, is then secured to the lower rim of the wrest plank f by means of the screws k. This being done, the adjustment of the strain is effected by suitably adjusting the height of the blocks i and by inserting between the framework and the soundboard on the one hand and between the soundboard and the metal frame on the other hand the spacing blocks *n* and *o*. The blocks vary the distance between the metal frame and the top of the soundboard bridges. The mounting is finished by screwing into the framework *a* the screws *h* through the edge of the metal frame *c*, the mounting frame *g* and the blocks *n* and *o* ; lastly, the upper part of the metal frame *c* is fixed on to the upper rim of the wrest plank *f* by the top row of screws K. All the elements are dismountable and may be readily replaced, for a given type of piano, by other similar elements made in standard types.

Some English makers have patented similar suggestions. One recent patent protected a device for adjusting the downbearing by permitting the raising or lowering of the hitch-pin plate.

All piano makers seem to be attracted by the soundboard as a field for invention, largely, without doubt, because the laws governing the bellying of certain musical instruments have never been tabulated. A writer, discussing the wonderful productions of the early Italian violin makers said: "The masterpieces of that period were not constructed upon an exact or scientific system, but were products of development of a traditional craft working upon empirical lines...... Careful historical research has revealed no record of laws or rules by which the great makers worked."

But no one can fail to understand that, while laws may remain undiscovered, they exist and operate ; and therefore a sympathetic hearing should be given to all suggestions concerning the soundboard of the piano, for it is the experimenter who will first achieve the desired results, and who will then lead to an elucidation of the causes of those results.

DOWNBEARING.

Freedom and purity of tone are largely dependent upon a good contact between the string and the bridge. Where the construction is such that some strings press too much on the bridge—for example, due to inequalities of tension—their neighbours press too little. The result is that one of the causes of falseness of tone is put into operation.

Downbearings of an instrument are spoken of in fractions of an inch ; but the point so often missed is that the bearing on the unstrung piano can be very different to that attained when the full pressure of the strings is exerted. A straightedge may be nearly one-eighth of an inch above the hitch-pin plate when rested on the top and bottom bridges of the piano which is not strung. Yet when the full tension is given, there may be no bearing whatever. Some boards yield under a light pressure : the ribbing, the nature of the wood, and the method of filleting (also the quality of the craftsmanship) accounting for the wide variations. A clinometer can be employed to register the angle of downbearing, which is the difference between the two angles made by (a) the speaking length and the horizontal and (b) the lower dead length and the horizontal.

The tangent of the downbearing angle multiplied by the string tension gives the down-pressure in pounds. The downbearing angle may be as great as $1\frac{1}{2}°$.

The persistent failure to obtain a good tone in sections of the compass in certain models is not infrequently due to irregular downbearing,—in the finished piano. Some markers-off will insist upon giving the bridge an appreciable slant towards the hitch-pin plate, leaving it a little "proud" to the wrest plank. This is unnecessary, for the down-pressure will bring the strings very nearly to a straight line—when the instrument is tuned. It is considered good practice to graduate the bearing angle to compensate for the greater flexibility of the centre of the board.

The strings of a violin cross the bridge at a comparatively sharp angle, and one might suppose the downbearing to be considerable : yet the reverse is the truth. Due to the very low tension of the strings[27] the pressure exerted on the bridge is about 23 lb.

As in the violin, so of course in the piano, and the higher the string tension the higher the pressure on the bridge. A tension of 160 lb. under ordinary conditions of manufacture gives a down-bearing pressure of about 5 lb. This would approximate half-a-ton over the whole soundboard, and is not excessive or detrimental. The danger, it is often found, lies the other way ; for, with a high string tension, a very small bearing is given. Any subsequent sinking of the board gives a tonal falseness and a general deterioration ; the adhesion between the steel and the wood is lost, and the strings are only held down by the rake of the pins.

Some years ago a "soundboard tension-resonator," named the Gertz, was patented in America. Fig. 110 shows the soundboard rim (K) and tension rods (E) of this device. It was claimed that by tightening up the rods at (F) the original arched form of the

[27] One authority gives the following figures for the normal tension of violin strings. G 23 lb., D 18½ lb., A 14 lb., E 12½ lb. Angle of bearing 20° ; downpressure, 23 lb. in all.

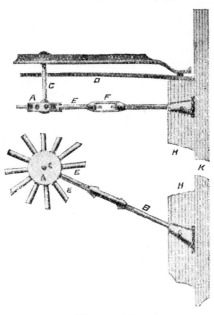

Figure 110

soundboard could be restored when age or other influences had caused a sinkage.   The downbearing could be increased or decreased at will.   Radiating from the centre-piece (A), the rods could be screwed up simultaneously to bring pressure on the entire board; or individually if any part of the soundboard had sunk and the bearing lost.

Mason & Hamlin grands were fitted with this plan for maintaining the bearing between the strings and the belly.   The word "resonator" does not, of course, describe accurately the device. To obtain a complete idea of this suggestion, it may be said that the soundboard-rim to which the soundboard is fixed can, by tightening up the tension screws (F), be drawn in slightly in all directions, which enables the arch of the belly to be controlled. But this is only possible with an elliptically-shaped surface, for any joints at corners would be destroyed by such abnormal stresses.   Upright pianos fitted with elliptical soundboards are not novelties, and the only difficulty is in the suitable attachment of the belly to the back.

There have been other ingenious plans to sustain or vary the resistance of the board against the downward pressure of the strings: in one, the invention of an Englishman, the bridge was channelled, and thus an up-bearing or pressure created. The "dished" belly (instead of the usual "buck" or camber), in which the bars were glued on the front and the strings passed through studs, was another means of giving an upward pull. It is not surprising that these last suggestions failed, because during the whole life of the piano the strings would be endeavouring to lift the bridge away from the board: the pull may have been as much as a ton. The fibres of spruce give way fairly easily, and screwing would not alone hold down the bridge.

Messrs. Ibach at one time made soundboards which were supported by steel springs. A recent German patent covered what might be called a combined up and down bearing stud for the soundboard bridge, this stud providing the only contact between the strings and the wood. There were two hitch-pin levels, one hitch-plate being a few millimetres above the other, and the strings running alternately from the stud to the lower level and then to the higher. One string pressed against the upper bearing of the stud and the next against the lower bearing: thus there were compensating strains, and it was claimed that the vibrations were enlivened thereby and that there was no deterioration.

There is no doubt that excessive downbearing destroys the responsiveness of any soundboard, the tone becoming "short" and "tight."

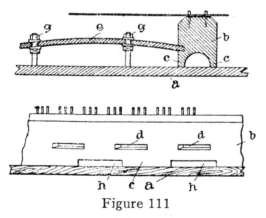

Figure 111

Attempts to increase the volume and duration of tone by using double soundboards, connected by posts or otherwise do not seem to meet with success. The double soundboard applied to the piano gives a muffled tone.

Mr. Emanuel Moor, some three or four years ago, patented a modified form of double-belly. Fig. 111 is taken from the original specification. The bridge (*b*) was grooved (*d*) to give contact to a secondary vibrating surface (*e*), which was supported by (*g*). It will be seen that the bridge (*b*) could be hollowed (see *h*), to give a lighter and more responsive contact with the main board (*a*).

VARNISH.

The penetration of varnish used by piano makers to seal up the natural resins of the soundboard wood is very slight. The oil varnish used by violin makers is, they claim, able completely to penetrate the maple and pine of the back and belly, and to be visible inside. These oil varnishes are very slow-drying, while the piano soundboard varnish has a large alcohol content, which is the solvent and which is a very rapid evaporator. The creamy-white streaks sometimes seen on soundboards is due to the work having been carried out in a cold, damp atmosphere; the alcohol has a strong affinity for water and the gums seem to coagulate.

It is very doubtful if the varnish adds anything to the resonant qualities of the board. But it retards decay of the structure and improves the appearance: in short, it is a preservative.

CHAPTER XII

The Piano of the Future

" Music is never stationary: successive forms and styles are only so many resting places, — like tents pitched and taken down again on the road to the ideal."
FRANZ LISZT.

A WORK of art is a sensitive creation which has a perfect, delicate and necessary finish. The friction of years does, of course, make some alterations in musical instrument construction, but the process is gradual: indeed, it seems that the greater the work of art, the less the passage of time is felt.

Attempts at improvements in musical instruments often display a mistaken sympathy for what is imagined to be the limitations, the defects, and the sufferings of an instrument in its original state. To remove a defect from an instrument is, frequently, also to remove a quality, because the musician by instinct seeks to turn a defect, or a limitation, into a definite quality. It follows that the greatest danger accompanying improvements is that of misinterpretation. Compositions which produce a designed effect in the old form of construction will produce an uneven balance, will accent weaknesses, and will be twisted and distorted when played upon the new instrument.

Thus attempts at a development of the piano must be chastened by a spirit which is the reverse of revolutionary. This spirit must be sympathetically disposed to old habits and customs: it must seek to explore new ideas tentatively. If tedious and tiresome instrumental defects are to be removed, the revolution must be of the pale pink order rather than of the blood-red. We are often reminded of "the defects of our qualities:" those who would give us a new type of piano—a new creation in art—need to remind themselves continually of the quality of the defects of the present instrument.

It is not unlikely, therefore, that new forms of piano con-
177

struction will offer, first, the piano in its existing state; and, second, the amplified mechanism.   The additional keyboard, pedals, or whatever form the improvement takes, will be independent: for, paradoxical though it may seem, the piano being so complete, new forms of construction all tend to amplification.

Before suggesting the actual shape which the new piano may take, it is helpful, first, to consider the influence of both the early keyboard instruments and the present piano on modern music.

A salient characteristic of the keyboard instrument is its *mechanical* nature.   A tablature, such as the staff notation, denotes a vastly different principle in the mind of a performer using the keyboard to that of a singer, a violinist, or a horn player.   By the use of a tablature, a distinct mental process is eliminated.   A violinist is under the obligation of imagining a sound before he can produce it, from which it is to be seen that *the keyboard is a labour-saving device*.   Now, the keyboard is very ancient and was first used with the organ.   Organ technique assumed sustained sounds.   The harpsichord and its precursors were quite different: the string once struck, the sound died away.   The result was that the stringed instrument which possessed a keyboard enabled the musician to indicate (though not to sustain) a very large number of notes.   Though these advantages over the organ were partly mechanical, there was undoubtedly also an artistic value.

The early application of music in all countries was to religious worship.   In England, the church educated boys for choral work.   Doubtless many remained with the church, but it is a fact that others, disliking the discipline, broke free. It was from this class that the minstrels were recruited. These men possessed some knowledge of the rudiments of music.   Their influence upon musical development was immense. The minstrels travelled from court to court, castle to castle, during the period which saw the introduction of the keyboard.

The keyboard instrument is an instrument of percussion. The initial impact of hammer and string is violent.   Compare it for a moment with the perfect instrument of musical sound production, the voice !   The piano of to-day is much less a percussion instrument than the clavichord:[28] the impact is less violent, and

[28] It is not always realised by those who have not studied the harpsichord that it had a fixed quality and degree of loudness due to the limit of elasticity of the string and of the quill which plucked it. The clavichord was, by way of contrast, capable of nice gradations of tone and many beautiful effects could be obtained. The clavichord held its own right through the spinet period and for some time after the introduction of the piano.

is given with a hammer instead of with a tangent. Yet there is
still a *noise* accompanying the tone.

It is a nice controversy: the question whether the psycho-
logical effect of the initial impact constitutes a defect of the piano
or otherwise. True, it may be a fault, because of the dispropor-
tionate violence that is required to produce the sound. Then,
again, the undue penetration of the sound is often objectionable.
Is it necessary for the piano to assume the characteristics of
bells and drums, which are used for secular purposes because
they carry and are perceived clearly above the hum of subsidi-
ary noises?[29]

In spite of the gradual standardisation of the orchestra during
the seventeenth century, musical historians consider that it was
the keyboard instrument which, during this period, dominated
the composers' work. And why? Because a percussion instrument creates a rhythmic impulse: it provides stress and accent.
(The voice, in contrast, produces accent by diminution or variation of quantity and quality.) Music of the fifteenth and sixteenth
centuries was confined largely to the lute, or the virginal:
but to - day the pianoforte is the dictator. And, if it is an
accepted fact that instruments are invented because composers
want them, it has also to be accepted that piano music is the
mirror that reproduces musical art of to-day. ·

We are told by competent authorities that the piano is the
instrument of the romanticists. It suited the romantic composer
because it awakened associations. Romantic music is saturated
with association. The piano can give the ecclesiastical atmosphere almost as well as the organ: it provides those poetic
visions of the German forest, the march of military men, wild
waves in arpeggios: in short, the piano can imitate all the
theatrico-musical effects, all the *Türkische Musik* the composer
can desire. One player at a piano can suggest a huge range of
orchestral instruments. Beethoven himself was acutely aware of
the usefulness of the piano in suggesting orchestral effects,
though obviously he was concerned with deeper things than
these.

[29] It is a fact only too true that the inferior pianos of to-day can be heard
at a very great distance. This is due, among other things, to the common
and very hard nature of the hammer felt. Listening from a distance, each
treble note stands out stark like a blow on a tiny bell: there is more noise
than tone: and the noise is not only tinny but is china-like in quality. Rapid
progressions on such pianos sound like the din of washing up crockery coming from the bowels of a large hotel. On a beautiful instrument, a rapid progression can yield the suggestion of even strings of exquisite pearls.

Passing to the possible avenues of piano development, it is necessary to be reminded that in some quarters there is a strong, if not a violent antipathy to the instrument. The dominating influence of the piano is considered in these quarters a positive danger. Objection is taken to its fixed tone: its rigid fixture to one temperament. Then it is said that its facility for animation (especially when operated automatically) tends to vulgarise stress and rhythm. It possesses all the dangerous possibilities of a "corner man" in a poor cinematograph orchestra. More than this, it overshadows the voice as a natural and normal method of producing music; and besides creating false values in sound-quality, it engenders an indifference to sustained melodic writing and limits the music lover's power of thinking in musical sounds.

✳   ✳   ✳

The "improvements" which must not be allowed to develop in the piano are those which would add to its usefulness to the variety artist. Another limitation is that of temperament. For good or evil, it seems that all keys must be equally slightly removed from truth. The simpler keys could of course be favoured, but this merely makes the distant keys impossible and prevents modulation. The "Wohltemperirtes Clavier" has stood the test of over three centuries.

Mechanical expressiveness might lead piano makers to con-vert the piano into such a chamber of horrors as an American cinematograph organ,— veritable man-traps. For example, the "beating of wings" and the flapping-fan effect of the cheap reed organ, or even chimes of temple bells.

Certain features in the piano as we know it to-day call insist-ently for improvement. Some of these defects may be indicated.

Bass Tone.—The notes of the extreme bass from about E^8 downwards are frequently mere noise, particularly on the short upright and on the 5ft. grand. (The lowest note written by Bee-thoven was the 16ft. C,—that is, the C^4 of the piano keyboard.) It is possible that, with a new metal (true, as yet undiscovered) these notes could catch something of the splendour and round-ness of horn tone. The $A\sharp^2$ on a modern concert grand has often a very fine and full musical quality.

Damping.—Can anything more suitable than felt be found for damping? Instantaneous silencing is required, and in the bass of uprights it is never obtained, not even with the best clip dampers.

Weak Trebles.—There are few pianos that have not a weak patch in the treble. Groups of notes can be painfully thin, so that the note can be only indicated rather than played.

Pedals.—The looseness and jerkiness of touch in those pianos which use the half-blow action demands improvement.

The Middle Pedal.—The individual-note sustaining pedal may be a complication, for, after all, we have only two feet. Yet it provides a refinement desired by many, and its embodiment ɪthe action would lead to a higher standard of action and touch regulation.

The more far-reaching possibilities of piano development must now claim our attention.

Touch.—A double-touch or any similar device has never made any appeal to the pianist. The small fixed depth of the descent of the key does not permit of any satisfactory alteration. (And it may be noted that, with this fixed degree of descent, there are some who claim to be able to employ as many types of "touch" as there are smells in an Eastern bazaar.)

Tone.—A complete tonal change attachment presents no difficulty to the piano manufacturer. Nor does it do so to the person called upon to use the device, which may be a pedal, a stop, or a button, for nothing more is required to vary the whole tone by the performers. The question to be asked is, Is this facility for tone variations desired? The clavichord or harpsichord effect is perhaps of some value in certain combinations. But the introduction of a small disc between the hammer and the strings—which is the general method of tone variation—is a small issue when compared with another suggestion sometimes made, that of providing the facility for striking the strings at a point other than at about one-eighth of the total length.

    ✳   ✳   ✳   ✳

Where, then, are we to look for improvements in the piano? Its percussive quality of tone cannot be altered. Its lack of ability to sustain sounds may offer a field for development. A very rapid and soft tremolo action might give the impression of continuity of sound to the ear, just as the cinematograph film gives the impression of continuity of movement to the eye. But is there not the danger of this continuity of sound leading to chaos?

As has been stated earlier, the piano is essentially a labour-saving instrument, and in this respect its influence upon musical art has been most felt.   It is the household orchestra, because it does the work—or, rather, it creates the impression—of the whole orchestra.   And is it not here that we stumble across the key to its future possibilities? The use of our elevated semitone is first credited to Guido d'Arezzo (995-1050), and it was developed very early in musical history, as the Halberstadt keyboards (1361) prove.   The present semitonal arrangement is merely a device to bring the existing scale within the stretch of the human hand. Does this device deserve extension?

Keyboards with *elevated tones*, instead of semitones, may be a first step in keyboard development.   The two (or more) manual piano may also have a place in the future. Uneven tonal balance is a real and crippling restriction to the present piano.   Four-hand harmony would come into its own as a double-manual instrument.

The difficulties of the supplementary keyboard or keyboards will not be mechanical, though there will certainly be consider-able difficulty in the ways of notation and technique, particularly if couplers are to be used at all extensively.

Dr. Oscar Bie, in his book, "A History of the Pianoforte and Pianoforte Players"[30] (the English translation of which is unfor-tunately out of print), makes some interesting comments on the probable development of the keyboard. It is suggested that the present arrangement of the keys—the sacred tradition of centuries —will pass in favour of the terraced system.   The flat keyboard gives the most natural expression of melody, but it makes the keyboard a C major keyboard, the tones outside this scale becom-ing subordinate.   Dr. Bie goes on to point out that since the seventeenth century musical conceptions are harmonic rather than melodic.   We can hear vertically as well as horizontally.

It was in the year 1882 that Paul von Janko constructed a key-board of six tiers, one above the other.   On this keyboard, tenths and twelfths can be produced with extreme ease, the finger reach-ing up or down to the range above or below the notes along which the hand is travelling.   Arpeggios through the whole compass of the keyboard can be given by a sweep of the wrist.   The Janko keyboard was improved by Paul Perzina (of Schwerin, Germany),

[30] The translators of this work make the strange remark that Dr. Bie, writing for the German public, used a more philosophic style than would be generally intelligible to the English reader !

and the Janko-Perzina keyboard with a single leverage to the key is shown in Fig. 112 :—

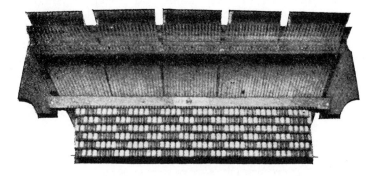

Figure 112

The Emanuel Moor duplex coupler piano (covered in this country by Patents 161,549 and 180,633) must be mentioned here. A number of these instruments have been made by the Æolian Company at Hayes. Fig. 113 shows the hands of a

Figure 113

performer at the Moor double keyboard. This new instrument offers first the piano in its existing form, but, if desired to be so used, it also offers an additional keyboard and couplers. The extra keyboard is in immediate contact with the first, and each white key of the first and lower keyboard has a little hummock at the back which rises to the level of the black keys and forms a convenient step to the upper keyboard. (See Fig. 113.) Fig. 114 shows the setting out of the two keyboards and explains that the upper range (B) is an octave above the lower (A). A third pedal, when down, makes everything played on the lower board doubled in octaves. There is, of course, only one action

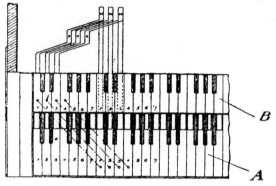

Figure 114

and one set of strings. Fig. 114 shows a tremendous key-splay, but the writer, having examined one of the keyboards, found that the splay was actually only half that shown in the figure, it being

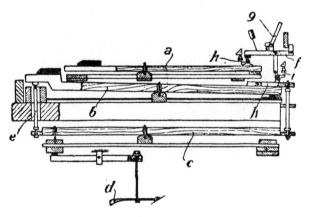

Figure 115

divided between the two sets of keys. There is a unique method of escapement for the keys (see Fig. 115), for one action wippen can be lifted from two sources, and it is essential that the operation shall be quite free and independent.

Explanation of Figure.

" In Fig. 115 a is a key of the upper keyboard and b a key of the lower keyboard of a piano having two keyboards. Corresponding keys of the two keyboards are arranged in line, but are adapted to strike notes distant from one another by an octave. For this purpose, the levers of the lower keys are oblique. Similarly, the levers c of the coupling mechanism are arranged obliquely, and each is actuated by a key distant by one octave from the key corresponding to the wire caused to be struck by the said lever.

" The coupling mechanism is put into operative position by means of a pedal d adapted to lift the lever c. The coupling mechanism may be then actuated by any of the keys b, by means of a pusher e. The wippen f of the mechanism of each hammer may be actuated either directly by one of the keys a or by a lever c of the octave coupling mechanism. On the said wippen f, is pivoted a jack g, which acts upon the hammer.

" Automatic escapements h, i are inserted between the keys a, b, and the lever c, on the one part, and the wippens f on the other part. By this means, when a note is struck, the wippen is automatically released from engagement with the striking key a or b or coupling lever c, and it is possible again to operate the said wippen from another key even whilst the key first struck is still depressed. Both the key b and the lever c act, as represented, upon the same intermediate striker k which is pivoted to the key b. Thanks to this arrangement, only one actual escapement mechanism is necessary for the key b and the lever c."

In the earlier notes on the possible forms which the modern piano may eventually take, mention was made of the Janko keyboard and the Moor double manual, but who can say if these new "vertical" keyboards and double manuals will find a place in the future? There are some who say that the principle admits of extension, and that we may see as a permanent fixture in the concert halls a gigantic triplex-coupler piano with two sets of hammers and strings, and with a third lower manual an octave below the normal.

There must, however, be one quality of tone only, for piano tone is as characteristic as the possibilities of the instrument are immense, and attempts to blend the piano with most other instruments are doomed to failure. A variety of cembalo stops, it is true, may make the piano more useful in combination.

There are two further suggestions for the development of the piano which deserve some attention before conclusion. First, the idea of Mr. Kaikhosru Sorabji to build a great tuning-fork piano, — very large forks "with a marvellous beauty of tone, volume and sustaining power" being used. These forks, he suggests, could be, by electric means, magnetised and sensitised. Further, it is proposed to adapt to this piano the Janko keyboard. Mr. Sorabji has expressed himself strongly about the neglect by modern composers and pianists of the Janko keyboard. We feel compelled to quote a paragraph :—

" Such, however, is the strength of vested interests, the combined apathy, stupidity, and mental laziness of ninety-nine out of a hundred musicians, that this wonderful invention (the Janko keyboard) which opens up unheard-of possibilities in the executional and compositional technique of the piano, which facilitates enormously the requirement of technique of an excellent order and vastly lessens the drudgery and soulless slavery that repels, and quite rightly repels, many gifted with imaginative musicianly sensibilities, but who lack the stupidity of those who imagine that genius is an infinite capacity for giving pains—to other people—who might otherwise have had a chance of developing into charming and sensitive musicians ; such, in fact, is the stupidity of musicians that this invention might as well never have been, for all the effect it has had."

It may be mentioned that Mustel of Paris, some fifty or more years ago, introduced the Typophone, which was an instrument built upon this tuning-fork idea. It was, however, probably for reasons of cost, supplanted by the Celesta, in which we have as a sound-producing medium a metal plate suspended over a resonating chamber. It is held that the tone of the Typophone was far superior to that of the Celesta, it being purer, clearer, and having more volume and body.

The last development towards a new piano which we have to mention is the idea of using two keyboards to produce quarter-tones.

The firm, August Förster, of Löbau, Saxony, about two years ago, made a quarter-tone horizontal instrument which was in effect two grands, one placed immediately over the other, the upper being tuned half a semitone higher than the lower. One set of strings and one soundboard only were used.

The two keyboards of this piano were so arranged that the hand could pass from the lower to the upper manual with ease: and to assist this a further manual existed at the back of the lower range. This third keyboard was at the same pitch as the lower range and could be described as an extension of the keys of the normal keyboard.

It is said that the Czech composer, Haba, has achieved considerable success with the new instrument; but it is not clear whether this composer has used the complete quarter-tone arrangement, or whether only eight shades of tone have been added to the octave, giving, presumably, a diatonic arrangement to the additional keyboard of the instrument, and twenty quarter-tones in all, instead of our normal twelve semitones.

Another suggestion which was recently patented in Germany is that a grand piano shall be constructed with two soundboards, two scalings, and two hammer systems, operated from one keyboard; the additional soundboard and strings are to be below the main body of the instrument, the depression of a key actuating two hammer systems. Messrs. Broadwood, a year or two ago, were working on an interesting form of construction for a small piano. This instrument, also, has two actions and two scalings, so that one key agitates six strings; and it may be that out of all these suggestions a maker will one day build a satisfactory single or double-scaled piano with one quarter-tone keyboard. But unless the new arrangement can be built into an upright piano as well as into a grand, it will have small chance of becoming popular. (The last two suggested forms of construction are not, of course, intended for the quarter-tone system.)

Another arrangement for a quarter-tone piano to be mentioned is the device of joining two grand pianos together and having two actions and two soundboards but one *double* keyboard. The difficulties of manufacture are immense, though the firm Grotrian-Steinweg, of Brunswick, have made such an instrument, as the following quotation shows:—

"In effect, this instrument (made by Grotrian-Steinweg) is really two ordinary grand pianos joined together, one of them being tuned a quarter-tone higher than the other. Both pianos are played by means of one keyboard with three sets of keys—black, white and brown—the brown keys comprising the quarter-tone scale. This special keyboard contains twenty keys in the octave instead of the usual twelve. By an elaborate system of levers it is possible to play in the ordinary way on the normal part of the piano or on the quarter-tone part, or on both sections together, thus producing combinations of inexhaustible variety."

It is said, however, that the touch is very heavy. Perhaps one day we may have the suggestion that these new instruments shall be operated by electro-pneumatic means, though this would

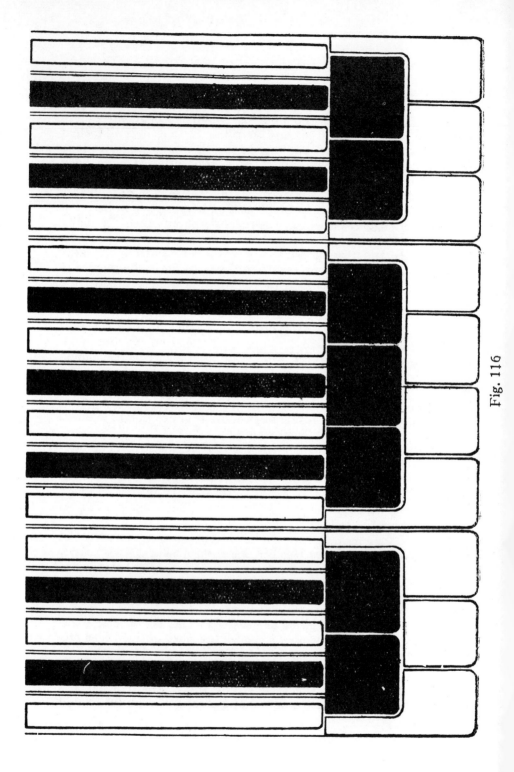

Fig. 116

infer the throwing overboard of all our present ideals of touch variation.

We may, however, permit ourselves the luxury of imagining an electric player attachment fitted to one of the large permanent three-manual instruments suggested by Mr. Sorabji. The performer's work would, we suppose, be limited to following the expression indications on the roll and pulling out the necessary couplers, though, no doubt, this too could be done automatically.

A German technical paper has given an illustration of an arrangement which shows, seemingly, twenty-four keys all within the normal span. Fig. 116 shows an octave of the keyboard built on these lines. To bring twenty-four keys, giving a complete quarter-tone scale, within the span of the hand is a very great achievement, and some information as to the exact dimensions and as to the quality of touch of this keyboard would be very welcome.

CHAPTER XIII

Notes on Musical Pitch

THE literature of musical pitch would fill a library. The chief feature about these never-ending loquacions is that they lead nowhere : they are the *cul-de-sac* of musical literature. The following table, which shows the historial aspect of musical pitch, is interesting :—

1361	Halberstadt organ.[31]	Frequency of treble A : 505·8
		(key No. 49)
1640	Vienna organ	... 457·6
1666	Worcester Cathedral organ	... 437·1
	By Thomas and Renatus Harris	
1788	Windsor : St. George's Chapel organ ...	... 427·8
	Measured by Ellis, February 1880, while still at mean tone temperament	
1828	Sir George Smart's Fork	... 433·2
1859	Paris Conservatoire ("diapason normal")	... 435
1878	Kneller Hall Military School	*circa* 452·9
1879	London : Erard's concert pitch ...	... 455·3
1885	London : International Exhibition ...	... 452
1896	Low or New Philharmonic pitch ...	... 439
1920	American Federation of Musicians ...	... 440

[31] See page 144 and Fig. 89 (page 143).

TUNING FORK

The convenient pitch carrier of to-day is a two-pronged fork of finely-tempered steel. Its main feature is that when set down against a suitable resonator it yields a simple tone ; there are no harmonics.

For the information of those who might wish to vary slightly the pitch of any one fork, the following facts are mentioned. Filing a little off the tips of the prongs of the fork raises the pitch, because the vibrating length is reduced. To lower the pitch of a fork, file the bottom *between the prongs :* this lengthens the prongs and lowers the frequency per second.

Messrs. J. & J. Goddard of London sell a set of twelve forks, two forks (A and C) for each of the standard pitches as we know them to-day :—

	Double Vibrations per second	
Old Philharmonic	A 454	C 540
British Army	A 452·4	C 538
Medium	A 444	C 528
American Federation	A 440	C 523·3
New Philharmonic (1896)	A 439	C 522
Diapason Normal	A 435	C 517·3

SEMITONE MULTIPLIERS

Starting with any given pitch number, a complete pitch table may be built up by means of the following multipliers :—

1·05946	1·49831
1·12246	1·58740
1·18921	1·68179
1·25993	1·78180
1·33484	1·88775
1·41421	2·00000

To find the number of vibrations for C corresponding to a given A fork, multiply the vibration number of the latter by 1·18921. For example, A 439 × 1·18921 = C 522.

To understand at a glance the difference in pitch between the various standards, the tempered vibration rates at the lowest pitch of the notes forming the octave: A^{49} and A^{61} are given below.

Note Number of Piano Keyboard		Vibration Rate at Diapason Normal { approx. to nearest whole number
49	A	435
50	A♯	461
51	B	488
52	C	517
53	C♯	548
54	D	581
55	D♯	615
56	E	652
57	F	691
58	F♯	732
59	G	775
60	G♯	821
61	A	870

It will be seen that the distance between Diapason Normal and the highest pitch now in use (Old Philharmonic, A 454) is less than a semitone. The difference, at the pitch of A^{49} between the highest and lowest pitch standards, amounts to about 19 double vibrations per second. (At the pitch of C^{52} the difference is 23 vs. per second.) The increase in the vibration rate between A^{49} and $A♯^{50}$ amounts to 26 vs. per second (as shown in the table above). Thus the difference between the Diapason Normal and Old Philharmonic standards is about two-thirds of a semitone. This may be small, but it is a handicap to the advancement of music.

THE MUSICAL MUSEUM

"A unique collection of unusual instruments"
Illustrated London News

The exhibits include reproducing pianos and organs which play music exactly as it was played by the great recording artists early in this century as well as:

Street Organs and Pianos	Self-playing Violins with
Musical Boxes	Piano Accompaniment
Nickelodeons	Orchestrions
Square Pianos	Barrel Organs
Dulcimers	Phonographs
Piano with 2 Vertical	Scale Model Piano
Keyboards	Orchestrelles

Welte and Wurlitzer Reproducing Pipe Organs
Aeolion Duo-Art Pipe Organ (in restoration)

ENTRY: Visits take the form of a guided tour, with the various instruments explained and demonstrated. MUSEUM COUNTER: During opening hours, after tours, visitors may purchase a wide variety of records, postcards, slides, music rolls, and books on musical instruments and their restoration. PRIVATE: Researchers, students and others may be given interviews by appointment, though a fee is usually requested, since the Museum receives little public subsidy.

In Temporary Premises at

368 High Street, Brentford, Middlesex.   01–560–8108

The 'Brabo'

One of the Weber Brothers' instruments in the Frank Holland Collection, now registered under the Department of Education and Science as the British Piano Museum Charitable Trust L. 242341, which may be seen during summer weekend afternoons in

The
MUSICAL
MUSEUM

Weber Brothers were established in Waldkirch in southern Germany in 1880 and made about 3000 instruments by the 1930s. The 'Brabo' instrument illustrated plays the piano with mandoline, violin, pipes and xylophone. Solo instrument effects can be obtained by switching. The piano is equipped with elaborate expression devices. Other instruments made were named: Unika, Grandezza, Erato, Violano, Euterpe, Isola, Venezia, Otero, Solea, Styria, Elite and Maesto.

UNWIN BROTHERS'

Music Instruments Series

A TREATISE ON THE ART OF PIANOFORTE CONSTRUC-
TION by Samuel Wolfenden. The original edition of 1916 together
with the supplement of 1927. Revised 1977. Including: Scale
Calculation, Scale Drawing, Contraction Drawing – Iron Frame,
Pattern Making, Sound-Boards, Tuning and Tuning Appliances,
Timber Seasoning, Glue and its Economical Usage, Pitch, Quality
of Piano Tone, etc.

PIANO TUNING by John S. Spice. Including: Preparation for
Tuning the Scale, Practical Tuning of the Scale, Tuning the
Treble Section, Falseness, Crank Control, Fine Tuning, Toning,
The Electronic Tuner, Mean Tone Tuning, Harpischord Tuning,
Customer Relationship, etc.

ANATOMY OF THE PIANO by Herbert A. Shead. An illustrated
dictionary and reference work. The names of individual parts of
the instrument are listed in alphabetical order and are cross
referenced where more than one term is used for the same part, or
where the function of one part can only be understood in relation
to another. Other terms essential for a full technical understanding
are also listed.

Please write for further details

UNWIN BROTHERS LIMITED
The Gresham Press
Old Woking, Surrey GU22 9LH